BLACK LEGACY PRESS™

WWW.BLACKLEGACYPRESS.ORG

Nigeria and its Tin Fields
By
Albert Frederick Calvert

ISBN: 978-1-63652-422-1

NIGERIA AND ITS TIN FIELDS

ALBERT FREDERICK CALVERT

PREFACE

The present conspicuous position which Northern Nigeria holds in the public eye is of very recent attainment, and its development has been, comparatively speaking, the work of a moment. The discovery of tin in paying quantities within its boundaries is the secret of its sudden leap to an eminence from which it compels interest, and attracts to itself more than ordinary curiosity and attention. It is with Northern Nigeria as it was with New South Wales and California, with the Malay Peninsula and Rhodesia. Their potentialities were admitted long before the existence of their mineral wealth was made known, but it was not until their minerals were discovered that they loomed into absorbing prominence.

The importance of Northern Nigeria as a British possession was demonstrated by the Niger Company; her possibilities as an exporter of cotton, rubber, and other vegetable products were early admitted; but it needed the revelation of her enormous alluvial tin deposits in the Province of Bauchi to attract to the development of her resources the capital and enterprise which alone can ensure the growth of a country's commerce.

But this sudden and surprising discovery also served to expose the widespread ignorance which prevailed in connection with our newest Protectorate, while it generated a desire for information concerning it. This little volume is put forward to satisfy this new-felt want, and it has, I think, the merit of being the first issued with that object. It has been compiled in haste, but care has been taken to verify the facts, and, as far as possible, the data has been derived from official sources.

I believe that no apology will be required for the illustrations, but for the use of the photographs from which they were produced I tender my grateful and sincere thanks to his Excellency Sir Walter Egerton, K.C.M.G., Governor and High Commissioner of Southern Nigeria; Sir William Wallace, K.C.M.G., late Acting Governor of Northern Nigeria; Mr. H. W. Laws, Engineer to the Niger Company; Mr. C. G. Lush, Consulting Engineer to the principal Nigerian Tin Companies; Mr. S. R. Bastard, Chairman and Director of several of the most important Nigerian tin mining companies; the Editor of the *Engineer*, Mr. R. Ernest Hope; Messrs. John Holt & Co., Ltd.; Mr. G. W. Christian; Messrs. E. H. Stein & Co., Ltd., and other prominent traders in Northern Nigeria.

A. F. CALVERT.

"Royston," Eton Avenue,
London.

CONTENTS

EARLY DAYS IN NIGERIA

In 1879, when Sir George Taubman Goldie organised the amalgamation of the rival trading firms of the Lower Niger and formed the United Africa Company, only a few far-sighted people could have had any idea of the possibilities of future commercial greatness that were possessed by this utterly unattractive and uncivilised region. "The Niger," as Colonel Mockler-Ferryman tells us, "was absolutely tabooed; its name was mentioned only in whispers, and the British public regarded it as an unlucky, pestilential spot, out of which no good could ever come." It must be remembered, in explanation of this pessimistic attitude, that all attempts to explore Nigeria and open up commerce on the river had failed more or less completely; a great number of lives had been sacrificed in successive expeditions, and no practical good had been accomplished. McGregor Laird, some quarter of a century earlier, had founded the African Shipping Company, with monthly sailings to the West African ports and, with the grudging co-operation of the Government, had contracted to keep a steamer on the Niger. But Laird died in 1857, when his spirited enterprise appeared to be on the point of yielding tangible results, and the country was still under a cloud when, twenty years later, the first organised attempt was made to develop its commercial resources.

THE PROTECTORATE PROCLAIMED

The United Africa Company's efforts were recognised by the grant of a Royal Charter in 1886, but its mission and its potentialities failed to appeal to the general public; and even when in 1900 the Territory, with its area equal to that of Germany and the British Isles combined, was added to the Dependencies of the Empire, the new Protectorate was regarded with indifference and suspicion as a present burden and a probable source of future trouble.

That was but a decade since, yet it was only the other day that Lord Crewe declared that "there is no part of the Empire about which higher hopes may properly be entertained than the Protectorate of Northern Nigeria;" and the Colonial Report, in emphatic corroboration of this optimistic opinion, asserted that "very few countries have witnessed such great changes for the better in such a short space of time, as has been the case with this Cinderella of the British Dominions."

It must be admitted that the Nigerias have been of late years more favoured in the matters of ocean transport and inter-communication. Since McGregor Laird started his monthly service to Lagos, the African Shipping Company has been succeeded by six shipping lines—the British and African Steam Navigation, African Steamship, Elder Dempster, Woermann, Hamburg-America, and the Hamburg-Bremen-Africa—the first three of which, to all intents and purposes, may be classed as Elder

Dempster's. Twenty-five liners and Elder Dempster's regular services call at Lagos each month—one nearly every day of the week. Two vessels of some four thousand tons are exclusively employed in bringing Welsh coal to Lagos; and a cargo service, another Elder Dempster enterprise, now runs from inside Lagos Lagoon to Hamburg, thus avoiding the transhipping of cargo in Lagos Roads or at Forcados. Persons who only know of Elder Dempster's famous service of ocean liners, which leave Liverpool every Wednesday and arrive at Lagos Roads sixteen days later, may be surprised to learn that they have a large and distinct inter-colonial service between Lagos and Secondi. These vessels, built of light draught to enable them to cross Lagos bar, not only afford shippers a short and rapid means of forwarding their produce, but are of immense service to the growing number of natives who travel, mostly for trade purposes, between Lagos and the smaller ports along the Gold Coast; while another Elder Dempster service runs weekly to and from Porto Novo in Dahomey and Lagos, carrying general outward cargo and bringing back produce for shipment to the United Kingdom and the Continent.

These services, which cater for the ramifications of the commercial activities of West Africa, are practically unknown at home, and the organisation and development of this enormous industry was, to a great extent, the work of one man—the late Sir Alfred Lewis Jones. It has been said of him that "when the story of our times comes to be written comprehensively, he will be bracketed with Cecil John Rhodes. One obtained a large territory for the Empire; the other enhanced immeasurably countries formerly judged as of questionable value. He was a pioneer in building up their commerce, and is of still higher estimate—he was instrumental in making them more fit to live in by revolutionising the health conditions." His varied commercial enterprises in West Africa are well known, and it is unnecessary here to enlarge upon them. They ranged from coaling and engineering companies with dry docks, to banking—which facilitated relations between the natives and the European traders—and included his cold-storage scheme, which the medical faculty admit has been one of the most powerful factors in lowering the mortality of West Africa. This object was also largely assisted by the investigations carried out at the Liverpool School of Tropical Medicine. The school was financed by Sir Alfred Jones, who also provided the means for putting the resultant discoveries into practice. He further established a branch of the School at Grand Canary, and arranged with Elder Dempster a cheap service from the West African Coast to the Canary Islands for malaria patients, whose lives depend upon their reaching that Mecca for invalids. By such means the dead merchant prince has lowered the death-rate among Europeans and natives in West Africa to a degree unthought of fifteen years ago, and he has built in that part of the Continent a monument to his name more enduring than brass, because the foundation was made for the betterment of his fellow-men.

THE NIGER COMPANY

But if the Elder Dempster Line have accomplished great things in establishing regular communication between England and the new Dependencies, much splendid pioneer work has been done in the country by the Niger Company. During the last few years they have opened up the Bauchi tin field in Northern Nigeria, and their trading and transport facilities have made it possible for them to carry out an enormous amount of development under great difficulties. The directors have had the courage of their convictions. In forwarding their own interests they have benefited the Protectorate, and if they have profited by their enterprise they have made the country a source of profit for others.

From the proceeds of the surrender of its charter to the British Government in 1900, the company were able to make a special distribution to its shareholders amounting to 145 per cent., and the sale of certain of their mining rights in the Bauchi Province has more than repaid them for the work that they had carried on in the district since 1902, and resulted in raising their dividend payment in 1909 from ten to twenty per cent. And in addition the Niger Company possess practically a monopoly of the transport to the tin fields, the value of which cannot be overestimated.

The Niger Company's share of the credit that is due for effecting this great improvement in the present condition and future prospects of the Protectorate may be at once admitted; but much has been accomplished since the control of the country devolved upon the British Colonial Office. In 1900 only some 30,000 square miles, out of a total of 250,000 in Northern Nigeria, were under some form of organised control. The remainder was controlled and ruled under conditions giving no guarantee of liberty or even life. To-day the whole condition of the country is entirely altered. Sixteen provinces, comprising the entire Protectorate, have been organised by the never-ceasing efforts of Residents, and the sum total of the unadministered area does not now exceed the 30,000 square miles that were under administration ten years ago.

PROGRESS OF SOUTHERN NIGERIA

At the date of the proclamation of the Nigerian Protectorates the Southern Colony was in a much more advanced state of development than its Northern neighbour, and was naturally regarded as the paramount partner. It had a sea border, a port at Lagos, which to-day is the most important town in West Africa, and it was destined to be the terminus of the first railway to be built in the new Dependencies. The markets and trading stations of the Niger Company were within its boundaries, the fertility of the soil was proved, its richness in rubber, tobacco, and coal was established, and its wealth of other vegetable products was well known. It is not at all surprising, then, that British pioneers and capitalists saw the splendid commercial future that was before Southern Nigeria, and were somewhat neglectful of the distant, isolated, and inaccessible Northern territories. Nor were they wrong, for the advance of its trade justified the most sanguine predictions, and, as will be seen by a glance at the appended tables (prepared in francs by Mr. C. A. Birtwistle, the Commercial Intelligence Officer of the Colony), its commerce to-day practically equals the total of the French Colonies of Senegal, Guinea, the Ivory Coast, and Dahomey:—

	All French West African Colonies. Imports and Exports. Value in Francs.	Nigeria. Imports and Exports. Value in Francs.
1899	116,843,000	78,000,000
1900	129,861,000	90,575,000
1901	131,459,000	96,625,000
1902	130,906,000	112,325,000

1903	161,819,000	111,700,000
1904	155,949,000	130,100,000
1905	152,471,000	128,775,000
1906	163,442,000	144,925,000
1907	177,436,000	192,550,000
1908	193,090,000	184,550,000

It will be noted at a glance that whilst French West African trade has increased by 65 per cent., that of Nigeria has grown by 136 per cent.

ANTICIPATIONS OF NORTHERN NIGERIA'S FUTURE

Northern Nigeria, however, was known to be rich in iron, and the existence of other minerals was suspected; its suitability as a field for the exploitation of the cotton-growing industry was realised and the British Cotton-Growing Association reported a few years ago that "in Northern Nigeria alone lies the possible salvation of Lancashire." Moreover, the Directors of the Niger Company had always foretold the ultimate importance that would be attained by the regions north of the Niger and the Benue. The company's trade flourished in the south, new products were being continually discovered and new factories opened, and the optimism of its shareholders was justified by the declaration of substantial dividends, but Sir George Goldie consistently predicted the boundless potentialities of the unopened North, and as far back as 1889 declared: "We can hardly impress too strongly upon our shareholders that our hopes of future prosperity rest far less on the lower regions of the Niger than upon the higher, inner, and recently explored country."

Sir Percy Girouard and others have warned the public against confusing Northern and Southern Nigeria, and running away with the idea that there is no great difference between them. As Colonel Mockler-Ferryman says: "Commencing with what is called the Niger Delta, we have a land of swamps and impenetrable forests, intersected by a vast network of streams and creeks and inhabited by numerous pagan tribes addicted to every species of vile custom, including even cannibalism and human sacrifices.... Above the pagan land—*i.e.*, at the confluence [of the rivers Niger and Benue] there is a marked change, not only in the type of the people but also in the nature of the country. Mohammedan influence commences to show itself, and low swampy wastes are superseded by rocky hills or far-extending grassy plains, well studded with magnificent trees."

NATIVE TIN WASHING

The existence of alluvial tin in these Northern regions was known for some considerable time, but until a year or two ago its value as a commercial asset was not seriously considered. Rumours of such sources of wealth frequently reached the Niger Company, and quantities of small faggots of very pure metal, which occasionally found their way down to the coast, afforded evidence that the natives had been working and smelting tin for a lengthy period. It was subsequently discovered that the procedure adopted by the native Nigerian tin miners, and described by Mr. Nicolaus, is as follows:

"The washers, usually working in gangs of three or four, wade into the river, tributary creeks and gullies, generally at or near some shallow rapids, and, loosening the gravel under water with a short hoe-like implement, scoop it into large calabashes about 18 inches to 24 inches in diameter. As soon as sufficient gravel is collected (about 30 lbs.), it is washed, and the resulting rough concentrate placed in a smaller calabash, 6 inches to 8 inches in diameter, and thoroughly cleansed, nearly all the fine tinstone being lost. The resulting 'black tin' containing the equivalent of from 60 to 65 per cent. metal, is sun-dried, and packed in bags and skins for transport to the smelting furnaces.

"This 'black tin' is usually smelted in various parcels on a royalty basis, exclusively by members of one family, who hold the process a profound secret. Only three native smelting furnaces are in use, and these are each capable of turning out about 2 cwt. of metal per diem. They are built of well-puddled clay, and are 3 feet 6 inches in diameter, and have at the back four tuyère holes conducting the blast from primitive sheepskin bellows to the hearth. The tin is reduced by means of charcoal, and runs through a channel 2 feet 6 inches long and 4 inches broad to a catch-pot, whence it is ladled by small gourds or calabashes and poured. The tin is cast in the form of thin bars of about an eighth of an inch in diameter and 12 inches long, which are produced by pouring the molten metal on semi-circular banks of clay, 18 inches high, perforated by dry Guinea corn-halms."

THE DISCOVERY OF BAUCHI TIN

The first actual discovery of tin in the Protectorate, or the first conclusive evidence of its actual existence there, has hitherto been 'wrop in mystery,' but, thanks to the courtesy of Sir William Wallace, late acting Governor of Northern Nigeria, I am in a position to dispel all uncertainty on the subject. In the course of a letter I received from Sir William, dated 21st October 1910, he says:—"Up to '84 we used to believe that the tin used by the Hausa people for tinning their brass ware was brought across the desert. I then, being busily engaged opening up the Benue River to trade, got a hint that the tin was being smelted in some of the Hausa States, and, on making inquiries, found that it was being produced in Bauchi. We did all possible to develop the trade in the tin straws, but with little success, as the pagan tribes would have no dealings with the Hausa merchants, and rightly so, as it would have only led to the subjection of the tribes to the Fulani, whom they kept at bay till our advent in 1902. Early in that year I went with the little army as Political Agent to subdue the Emir of Bauchi, and after settling that matter I was able to get messengers through to the Delimi River, close to the Naraguta, from whence they brought about a quarter of a hundredweight of the tin sands, the first ever procured or seen by Europeans. This sample I brought home, and submitted to the Directors of the Niger Company, who shortly afterwards took out a prospecting licence over 1000 square miles. Since then, thanks principally to Mr. Laws, the mining industry has slowly forged ahead, until the rush came along this year. Year in, year out, I have been urging companies and encouraging prospectors to come along until I almost despaired of success; but now, given a railway to the tin field, the industry cannot but prosper if the Government do not hamper it with too many restrictions."

THE NIGER COMPANY'S EXPEDITION

Sir William Wallace's tribute to the work done by Mr. Laws, the plucky and importunate mining adviser of the Niger Company, is entirely merited. The existence of paying tin was regarded with some scepticism. It has also been surmised that the officials and civil servants had too comfortable berths to risk the disappointments and discomforts of prospecting work. Moreover, the Niger Company was in a flourishing condition, and its directors were not anxious to launch into mining enterprises. But Mr. Laws and his assistants were indefatigable. In 1902 and 1903 three expeditions were despatched to locate the tin areas. The little party, under the protection of an armed escort—for at that time the natives, now so friendly, were somewhat hostile—proceeded to make a geological examination of the country east of the Niger, and eventually found tin in the Province of Bauchi, some 600 miles to the north-east of Lokoja. Further prospecting located the stanniferous area to the outlines of the Gura Mountains, a small range known as the Naraguta and Shere Hills in the Badiko district of that province.

THE FIRST GEOLOGICAL REPORTS

The geology of the area, as described by Mr. R. C. Nicolaus, is composed of granites, igneous intrusions of diabase and porphyry forming the prominent peaks of the hill range. Near the river a coarse grey gneiss forms a contact with the granite, both of which rocks are traversed by lenticles and gash veins of quartz, and several small igneous dykes cross diagonally the general strike of country, which is north-east and dips west.

Although the stream tin had so far only been prospected in the neighbourhood of the rivers, there was abundant evidence to show that the source of the tin supply came from a stockwork formation in the granite at the slopes and at the base of the foot-hills. A somewhat remarkable feature of this deposit was that a considerable quantity of metallic tin was discovered under the river banks during prospecting operations. It was found in small grains and nodules about the size of a bean, its surface very thinly coated with only a trace of iron. It was very ductile, and emitted, on crushing, the peculiar tin cry. Its mode of occurrence in the gravels, associated with coarse grains of stream tin at a depth of some 15 feet under the surface, did not at first allow its genesis being determinable, but it was unhesitatingly put down as "native tin"—a mineral up to that time of very rare occurrence.

FIRST SHIPMENT OF TIN

Mr. Laws and his engineers were so well satisfied with their work, and the results they produced were so encouraging, that the Niger Company applied in 1905 for a number of mining leases in selected areas. In spite of slight difficulties arising from a scarcity of water in the dry season, a considerable amount of development work was accomplished, and the company secured an output of one ton of black tin per diem. These results proved that the gravels could be worked profitably, while the geological structure of the country compelled experts to the conclusion that the field represented by far the most important discovery of native tin that had been made. Further examination of the district, which fully confirmed the expectations raised by the first reports, has inspired the prediction that this Northern Nigerian tin field is perhaps the richest in the world.

The Niger Company continued to treat the alluvial in the old primitive method, which consists in the main of the use of calabash and sluice boxes, by which they have, up to the present time, secured over 1000 tons of black tin. Still, the mineral resources of the colony were not, until recently, appreciated in accordance with the proved facts. Lord Scarborough year after year had told the British public, in his annual speech to the shareholders of the Niger Company, that there was treasure in Northern Nigeria in the shape of alluvial tin. He told them, in March 1907, that during the previous fifteen months roughly 240 tons of black tin, of the approximate gross value of £30,000, had been obtained from one property, the Naraguta, or an average of 16 tons a month. He told his shareholders in 1908 that the Niger Company had won £29,933 worth of tin for that year. Last year he said: "As regards tin development, we have brought home and marketed an increased quantity of ore compared with the previous year." This year the chairman of the Niger Company declared a 2s. dividend per share as a result of the sale of a small portion of their mining lands.

OFFICIAL INFORMATION ABOUT THE NEW FIELD

The first official recognition of the importance of the Bauchi tin deposits was conveyed to the public in the Colonial Report on Northern Nigeria in 1905, and in 1906 was published the First Report on the Results of the Mineral Survey of Northern Nigeria, 1904-5. "The mineral resource of Northern Nigeria being virtually unknown" (to quote the report), "a mineral survey of the Protectorate to be carried out under the general supervision of the Director of the Imperial Institute by surveyors nominated by him, was proposed by Sir F. Lugard, the High Commissioner of Northern Nigeria, and sanctioned by the Secretary of State for the Colonies in 1904." It was arranged that the officers of the Survey should spend about eight months of each year in Northern Nigeria in exploring the mineral deposits of selected districts.

In the general introductory summary of the first report of the surveyors, the prospects of the tin fields of Northern Nigeria are described with the customary official reserve. "Tin, in the form of cassiterite," the report stated, "has now been found in the stream beds of other districts. It is probable that as soon as suitable transport is provided Northern Nigeria will become an important tin-producing country. Already deposits in the Bauchi Province are being worked by the Niger Company, and the metal smelted on the spot. The first consignment of tin from the Protectorate has reached this country."

The prospect presented by this information, backed up by substantial shipments of tin, might have been expected to stimulate the curiosity of both prospectors and capitalists, and that other Richmonds would have made an appearance in the Bauchi field. But any hopes of such a result were doomed to disappointment. The Niger Company continued to win mineral, and the Mineral Survey persisted in their efforts to prove the extent of country over which the granites were tin bearing. It is possible that the remoteness and inaccessibility of the Protectorate operated unfavourably in the minds of mining adventurers, and the evil reputation which had been erroneously given to the country may have moved financiers to an excess of cautiousness. The colony made no new friends, and, as will be shown later, it was not until last year and then only by the accident of failure in another direction, that capital was diverted into the new tin field.

TINSTONE CONCENTRATES ANALYSED

Eleven specimens of tinstone concentrates from the Zagi River, south of Bauchi, from Bula, Tilde, and the river beyond Joss were forwarded to the Imperial Institute, and with only one exception were found upon analysis to contain tin in quantities of from mere traces up to 80.85 per cent, of tin oxide, equivalent to 63.5 per cent. of metallic tin in the concentrate.

The official general remarks on the specimens analysed were as follows:

"Most of the concentrates were obtained from the plateaux of Tilde, Rukuba, Joss, and Ngell. On the first three of these the principal surveyor reports that the Niger Company has prospecting camps. The finest grained tinstone is found on the Tilde plateau, the coarser material coming from Joss and Ngell. The tinstone is said to be irregularly distributed, and adjoining pits may furnish such different yields as 10 lbs., or less, and 400 lbs. per ton on gravel worked. The average yield at the Rukuba camp is 25 lbs. per ton. The present works, it is stated, are all in the near neighbourhood of the river Delimi, but it appears that the gravels are more or less rich in tin over the whole surface of the plateau. The river-beds in some cases contain valuable tinstone-bearing gravels, as is shown by the results of the analysis of the concentrate from the river-bed at Tilde, which contained 68 per cent. of tinstone. That from beyond Joss contained only 40 per cent. of tinstone, possibly owing to the difficulty of separating the ilmenite from the tinstone by washing. The concentrate from the Kende River consisted almost entirely of ilmenite. The presence of the latter mineral in the stream beds will introduce a difficulty in the concentration of the tinstone, as it is not readily distinguishable by inspection from tinstone, and collects with it in the first concentration.

"The results so far obtained show that tinstone is widely distributed in the province of Bauchi in the alluvium of both the high and low plateaux. As these tinstone districts are in process of being prospected, it is scarcely worth while to discuss the commercial value of the tin concentrates here, but it may be pointed out that several of these concentrates contain monazite, and this may be worth recovering. The amount of monazite present is usually small, and it is scarcely likely that its recovery under present circumstances would pay for the working of an electro-magnetic concentrator, which would be required to effect its separation. If, however, it becomes necessary to use such concentrators in order to separate the ilmenite, which occurs with the tinstone, then it would probably be worth while to recover the monazite as a by-product.

"The question of the origin of the tinstone occurring in this region is of great interest, and the officers of the Survey propose to devote further attention to the subject."

The Colonial Report for 1907-8 carried us no further, as the third Survey party which arrived in the country in December 1907 were still upon their seven months expedition, and the results of their work had not been received. The report referred, however, to the fact that the Niger Company, continuing its work on its licensed area in the Bauchi Province, were exporting black tin to the amount of 500 tons per annum, and added: "The main difficulty in the development of this promising industry is its situation. With the construction of the railway through Zaria it should be possible to place the mines in close connection with it by means of a road, which should also serve the Bauchi Province."

THE REPORTS OF EXPERTS

In one of his reports on the Bauchi tin area, Mr. Lush says:

"There is not the slightest doubt that before very long many of the deep alluvial flats that are some distance from the shallow and more easily worked tin ground will be worked. The values may turn out to be poorer than the shallow ground, but the natural facilities are better owing to the water supply being sufficient for continuous working without the expense of erection of dams. On the other hand, when you get out of the granite country, the further you are away from the source of the tin the greater are the impurities mixed with it. The numerous creeks, after passing through the schists and other rocks emptying into the main river, all tend to this, and titanic iron, tourmaline, rutile, and gem sand form a large percentage of the concentrates. However, if on boring, the deep ground turns out payable, there should be no difficulty in getting rid of the impurities and dressing the tin up to 70 per cent."

Mr. L. H. L. Huddart, writing on this subject in his report on the South Juga property, says:

"*Sources of the Tin.*—The black tin is probably derived from the granite of which it is a rock constituent, and from stock-works in the granite quartz porphyry occurs very similar to the 'elvans' in Cornwall.

"*Nature of the Wash.*—In the upper end the wash is a fine whitish granite, containing no large pebbles or boulders, and is near the original source of some of the Juga tin. The surface is slightly cemented with iron oxides in which cassiterite often grows. The whole wash very easily breaks down with water. The ground further down the property is similar except that the alluvial has travelled further, and consequently has been sorted to a greater extent.

"Taken generally, the tin bearing is the product of denudation from the granite of which the bed-rock, and sides of the valley are composed. The tin occurs in the wash right up against the granite on both sides of the valley. The topaz is abundant in the wash, and with some zircon and rootile is almost the only mineral besides cassiterite occurring in the concentrates."

In his report on the Kurdum River Tin Concession, Mr. Huddart says:

"*Geology.*—The base rock is a foliated gneiss and schist; the great granite *massif* forming the Jarawa Hills lies to the west of the property. There is a good deal of granite on the property, with some dolerite. The rocks are compact, and show considerable signs of regional metamorphism.

"*Source of the Tin.*—The tin has been carried down from the rich placers at the head water of the Kurdum River, and form feeders that come in above the property from the Jarawa and Fuersum country. In one or two places the natives work the river-bed, an indication in itself of high value, as it does not pay them to work any but rich gravel. The alluvial ground is a quartz gravel with sand near the top. There is very little clay, and long boulders are unlikely, and the wash is friable and easy to work. The river-bed gravel where coarse is very rich.

"*Concentrates.*—These contain usually minerals such as ilmenite, rootile, zircon, and some topaz and garnet. The tin is of good quality, and varies in colour from black to ruby and pale yellow. A little monazite is found, and an occasional colour of gold. There should be no difficulty in shipping concentrates that will assay 71 or 72 per cent. metallic tin. The tinstone is of a good average size for saving in the sluice boxes which can be given a good grade."

FRESH DISCOVERIES ANNOUNCED

The Government Report on Northern Nigeria for 1908-9 contained the announcement that tin in paying quantities had been located in the Provinces of Bauchi, Nassarawa, and on the Kobba-Ilorin border, and this information has since been supplemented by the Akerri (Nigeria) Tin Company Ltd., which has taken up a tin area in an entirely fresh district, one day's journey west of Zungeru, and one and a half day's journey north-east of Jebba.

Meanwhile, in a White Paper on "Nigeria, September 1910," issued in the following month of October, we get an official reference to the new tin industry:

"Mr. Parkinson states that in the Oban Hills, Southern Nigeria, there are tourmaline pegmatites, and Schmeisser has recorded that since the discovery of an apparently rich tin deposit near Banyo, there has been much prospecting for that mineral in the Cameroons. Surface tin is found in Northern Nigeria by the natives, and sold, chiefly to the Niger Company, but mines on a large scale have not as yet been worked. The geological surveyors sent out by the Imperial Institute have detected the presence of alluvial tin in many sand and river gravels. At Uwet, in Old Calabar, Mr. Parkinson reports the occurrence of tinstone

during the year 1906, and of the washed samples 80 per cent.
was tinstone, and the remainder was garnet, tourmaline, quartz,
and columbite."

CONFIDENCE IN THE FIELD ESTABLISHED

The Bauchi tin won by the Niger Company is of rich quality, and
commands a considerably higher price than ordinary English
tin; but while Lord Scarborough persistently told the public
of the results of their operations, mining was not energetically
proceeded with, and as has been said the new field attracted less
attention than it deserved. But as prospecting work in the district
became more general, it was realised from the virgin nature of
the area, the cheapness and abundance of labour available in the
district, and the enormous extent of the surface deposits, that the
regions were extremely valuable and presented potentialities of
great and continuous profits. In the face of this later information
the first feeling of scepticism with which the discovery was
received passed away, doubt yielded to confidence, and it was
soon known that some of the most astute and influential groups
in the City were interested in the exploitation of the new field.

But although the future of the Bauchi tin district was assured,
it was necessary for some one to be first in the systematic development of the new field. Every report emanating from the
colony confirmed the story of the richness of Nigerian tin, and a
Royal Colonial Institute address had admitted that "if the professional reports were anything like approximately correct and the
supply is regulated, a fabulous amount of wealth is waiting to be
extracted," but the opportunity to make fortunes out of Northern
Nigeria was neglected until the Champion Gold Reefs of West

Africa, Ltd., who had abandoned their gold property on the Gold Coast, boldly threw their remaining capital of £12,000 into the new field.

THE PIONEERS OF NORTHERN NIGERIAN TIN

The credit, therefore, for placing the Nigerian tin fields before the British investor is due to Messrs. Walter and Oliver Wethered, and Mr. S. R. Bastard. It was Mr. Walter Wethered, being impressed by the large quantities of metal which were being brought down by the natives and sold to the Niger Company, who formed the opinion that these fields might be suitable for working on a large scale. Having satisfied himself on this point he was able to induce Mr. Bastard, and his brother, Mr. Oliver Wethered, to join in the business, and as a result the Champion Gold Reefs of West Africa, Ltd., of which Mr. Bastard was Chairman, decided in the month of September 1909 to embark its remaining capital and all its energies in the exploitation of the new Nigerian tin field. In October the first members of their staff were sent out to the properties they had already secured, to be followed on 3rd November by Mr. C. G. Lush, the well-known tin expert, who was to advise them as to the best method of developing their properties. Everything that happened satisfied this pioneer group of the value of the field, and they formed the Tin Fields of Northern Nigeria, Ltd., which was registered on 7th October 1909, with a capital of £100,000. Mr. Bastard became chairman of this company.

The Nigerian Tin Corporation, Ltd., was registered on 14th October 1909, with a capital of £100,000. On this occasion Mr. Oliver Wethered took the chairmanship. No further company was floated during the year 1909, but on 15th January 1910 this same group issued the Naraguta (Nigeria) Tin Mines, Ltd., with a capital of £175,000. This company has already, in the few months it has been working, recovered over 300 tons of tin, and has declared its first dividend. The next venture to be floated by the Champion Gold Reefs company was the Northern Nigerian (Bauchi) Tin Mines, Ltd., registered on 2nd February 1910, with a capital of £200,000, of which Mr. Oliver Wethered became a director.

The foregoing were the first five companies registered for the sole purpose of working the alluvial tin deposits of Northern Nigeria, and they were all promoted by this pioneer group, comprising Messrs. Walter and Oliver Wethered, and Mr. S. R. Bastard. All these companies are doing excellent work, and showing good results. After February of this year others entered the field, and since March last a large number of companies and syndicates have been registered and formed, several of which are at work.

It was only to be expected that such brilliant results as these would have the effect of inducing the more conservative firms to enter into the fields of Northern Nigerian mineral enterprise, and now Messrs. Wernher, Beit, the Consolidated Gold Fields of South Africa, Fanti Consolidated, and many other leading groups of bankers and capitalists are represented in the Bauchi Province.

THE INACCESSIBILITY OF THE FIELD

But while the prospecting and actual mining work being done on the Bauchi field are establishing an ever-widening recognition of its mineral wealth, its inaccessibility and the difficulties of transport, which represent its chief drawbacks, have not yet been overcome, and it may be opportune to explain here the methods of transport employed in the two Nigerias, to describe the railway system, and to give some ideas of the difficulties of carriage with which the mine owners of Northern Nigeria have to contend.

Southern Nigeria, through which the Northern Protectorate is reached from the coast, is covered with a network of waterways, which are the natural transport roads of the entire region, and the Marine Department is continually surveying old and overgrown streams and opening up new river routes. It is possible, travelling by the Niger River from Forcados to the confluence at Lokoja, and following from that point the Benue River to Loko, to arrive within about 180 miles of Bauchi, or going by rail from Lagos to Jebba, the present northern terminus of the line, to get, as the crow flies, within 300 miles of that centre. The river route is obviously the quickest and cheapest, and is the one still in use, the natives carrying the tin in parcels of 60 lbs. weight on their heads from the field to Loko, travelling about 15 miles a day. At Loko, the metal is put into small steamers or barges, according to the season, and conveyed to the confluence, where it is transferred to Niger boats and taken to Forcados for shipment to Liverpool, the entire journey occupying thirty-five days and costing £29 10s. per ton.

COST OF TRANSPORT

When the construction of the Kano Railway from Baro on the Niger to railhead is opened, and the road connecting the railway to Bauchi is made, the journey will be appreciably shortened. The completion of the railway from Lagos in 1911 should further reduce it to about twenty-eight days, and again when motors are available on the new road, to about three weeks.

The cost per ton by the Forcados-Baro route will be:—

	£	s.	d.
By sea to Forcados	2	0	0
Forcados to Baro by boat and by train from Baro to railhead by cheapest rate	7	12	6
From railhead to tin field, about	9	0	0
	£18	12	6

This will be increased when the maximum rate is charged, and will be reduced when the motor transport on the new road is available.

THE RAILWAYS OF NIGERIA

The future cost and time of transport depends upon the completion of the railway construction at present in hand, and the decision of the Government with regard to the suggested new line to connect the tin fields with some selected spot upon the Baro-Kano line of railway. The Lagos railway to Jebba in Northern Nigeria is 307 miles in length, but although the last constructed stretch of 60½ miles from Ilorin was only opened in August last, the line has already been continued for some 50 miles beyond the Niger, and the balance of 70 miles to be completed to Zungeru, the capital of Northern Nigeria, is expected to be finished early in the coming year. By this route, when the connecting line from Zungeru to the Baro-Kano railway is constructed, and the branch from the latter railway to Bauchi is built, it will be possible to carry machinery all the way from Lagos to the new field by train, and bring the metal down to the port by the same service.

But although this Lagos railway, as it is still called, taps a fertile and thickly populated country and connects the capital of the north with the coast, it became, with the commencement of the new Baro-Kano line the second, instead of the first, most important factor in the development of Northern Nigeria. Until the year 1907 the Northern Protectorate possessed in the way of railways but one light 2 feet 6 inch tramway of 22 miles in length, which connected its capital, Zungeru, with Baro, the nearest navigable point on the river.

It was in May 1907 that Sir Percy Girouard, the Governor, whose name had already become famous in connection with his splendid railway work in the Sudan and in South Africa, formulated the railway policy, and recommended the construction by the Public Works Department of the Protectorate of a 3 feet 6 inch gauge railway from Baro, on the Niger River, to Kano, a distance of a little short of 400 miles, on an estimate of £3000 per mile. In August of the same year the Imperial Government sanctioned the construction of the proposed line.

At the same time the views of the administrative Southern Protectorate were met by the extension of the Lagos line into Northern Nigeria, with a connection to be established from Zungeru with the Baro-Kano railway, making it possible to travel from Kano either all the way by rail to the coast at Lagos, or by rail to Baro, and thence by river steamers to the mouth of the Niger. It is expected that the bulk of the exports will follow the line to Baro, and thence be carried to the sea by water transport, but the Lagos line serves such a rich and well populated country, that when the Port of Lagos has been rendered accessible by the harbour improvements now in construction, the line should prove of increasing economic value, quite apart from any trade it may attract from the more easterly provinces of Northern Nigeria.

NEW LINE ADVOCATED

The Baro-Kano railway was put in hand at an extremely opportune time, and it was while the work of construction was being rapidly pushed forward that the discovery of tin in the Bauchi Province turned the thoughts of railway construction in an easterly direction, and the continuous and consistently rich finds which rewarded the efforts of prospectors in this region called daily and hourly attention to its remoteness. At first it was considered that the formation of a good road from Bauchi to strike the Baro-Kano line about Zaria would suffice for the needs of the field, but the extraordinary extent and richness of the deposits, and the phenomenal success achieved by the Naraguta (Nigeria) Tin Mines, Ltd., the Lucky Chance Mines, Ltd., and other companies at work there, emphasised the self-evident fact that nothing less than a branch railway would be sufficient to adequately develop the new industry. London capitalists expressed their willingness to find the money to finance the new line, but the question was, and still is, under the consideration of the Colonial Office, and Sir Walter Egerton, the Governor of Southern Nigeria, and Sir Hesketh Bell, the High Commissioner of Northern Nigeria, and Sir William Wallace, the late acting

Governor of that colony, all strongly favour the construction of the line by the Government rather than by private enterprise.

SIR WALTER EGERTON'S OPINIONS

Sir Walter Egerton, in an interview he granted to a Press representative in June last, said: "Everybody believes the tin deposits to be very rich, and if only half the reports concerning them are true, there is more than enough to warrant the expenditure of making a branch to the tin fields of the Province of Bauchi. This would give direct access from the sea at Lagos to the tin fields. The reports show that the tin alluvial is similar to that of the Malay Peninsula, which produces more than half the tin of the world. Southern Nigeria has already lent the money required for the construction of the railway to Kano, and it is a question for the consideration of the Secretary of State whether we should not also finance the building of the line to the tin areas. I should think it would be a great advantage to Southern Nigeria to have such communication, as a large traffic might be expected. If the Secretary of State agrees, there is no reason to expect that there will be any opposition in Southern Nigeria to financing the line, for the success of the tin industry will have a wonderful effect not only on Northern, but also on Southern Nigeria, for the Protectorates, though two politically, are one geographically."

THE GOVERNMENT AND THE PROJECTED LINE

Since this interview was published it has been persistently rumoured that the Government have decided to build the suggested line from a point near Rigachiko, on the Baro-Kano line, to a place called Toro, between 120 and 130 miles distant, in the centre of the tin district, and midway between Naraguta and Juga. The country which the line would traverse has been surveyed, and a new road, 12 feet wide throughout, and capable of conveying light motor traffic in the dry season is being constructed, and will probably be completed before the end of the present year. But the Government have not yet announced their decision, and it is doubtful, although efforts have been made to induce them to divert the funds for extending the line from Zaria to Kano for the purpose of the tin fields branch, whether they can be persuaded to do so. It is believed, as Sir Walter Egerton said, that if the Government acts on the recommendation of the Governor of Northern Nigeria, the Government of Southern Nigeria would be willing to undertake the construction of the line, and should the Colonial Office decline to sanction the scheme, representatives of several of the companies interested in the new tin field have expressed their readiness to finance the railway.

As recently as October 22nd a meeting of representatives of the various Northern Nigerian tin companies was held at the London Offices of the Niger Company, when a general committee, to be named the Northern Nigerian Mines Association, was formed, composed of a representative of each of the companies, and a sub-committee, composed of Lord Scarborough, Mr. S. R. Bastard, Mr. O. Wethered, Mr. Godfrey, and Mr. Berry was appointed to deal with urgent business. The chief attention of this meeting was naturally paid to the question of transport, and the first business done was the passing of a resolution urging the Colonial Office to construct the railway to the Bauchi tin fields as early as possible. The Association decided on the appointment of a medical officer, and they have, furthermore, given instructions for a hospital to be built on the field at Joss. It will therefore be seen that everything possible is being done to urge upon the Government the importance of pushing forward this work, which will doubtless be taken seriously in hand before long.

VARIOUS OPINIONS

Everybody connected with the Protectorate or interested in the new tin field is agreed as to the absolute necessity of constructing the line.

Mr. J. Tomson, the chief engineer of the Anglo-Continental Mines Company, who recently returned to England after an extended tour in the Bauchi district, declared that the difficulties of transport are at present tremendous, but he is of opinion that they could best be overcome by running a railway from Minna, a point on the Baro-Kano line to Naraguta, the capital of Bauchi.

"Before I left," said Mr. Tomson to a representative of the *Morning Post*, "I had an interview with Sir Hesketh Bell, the Governor, and found him most sympathetic towards the mining industry. He recognises that the railway should be built to the tin fields as quickly as possible, but of course it is a question of ways and means. If the Colonial Office came to the rescue and made a special grant for laying the line, or else allowed the united mining companies to construct it themselves, which they are quite willing to do, all would be well. But it is important that something should be done at once. If not, there is going to be a serious difficulty over the food supply, because so many mining companies have gone to the Bauchi district that the farmers are unable to cope with the demand for food. With a railway to

Minna and then along the line now being laid to Zungeru, which connects up the Lagos railway and the line from Baro, the ore would reach port in a few days."

Mr. Beresford, the Secretary of the Administration of Northern Nigeria, in an official letter written to a correspondent, discussing new means of transport in the Protectorate, says:— "A survey for a road has just been completed, and it has been found that the Rishi Pass is not a practicable line, and it is considered that Toro or Tilde, and not Liruei, should be the point of objective. It is hoped that by December next a rough road, fit for carts or light motors, may be completed to Toro *via* the Gusu Pass, but the Governor is strongly of opinion that nothing but a railway will suit the requirements of the tin fields, even in the near future, and he hopes that it may be possible to find funds for such a project."

THE ROUTE DESCRIBED

When the work of seeing these pages through the press was nearing completion, a letter arrived at the London offices of the Tin Fields of Northern Nigeria, Ltd., from their engineer, Mr. Jerome J. Collins, describing the means of transport from the coast to the seat of operations in the Bauchi Province. The particulars, which are given from personal experience of the journey, are both interesting and instructive, as they are also the last word to hand on the subject, and the excerpts which follow are published by the courtesy of the directors of the company, by whom the letter was received.

Writing from Kogin Jarawa, under date September 13, Mr. Collins says:—

Niger River Transport.—Forcados to Baro.

The distance is 407 miles. The Niger Company, Ltd., and the Government run shallow draught steamers carrying passengers and cargo. The Government steamers run a weekly service in connection with the mail steamers from Liverpool. The Niger Company run steamers as inducement offers.

The time occupied is about ten days by both services, but a great deal of this time is taken up with stoppages at the various towns along the river.

The Government steamers are in a very bad state of repair, and much time is lost owing to breakdowns. In the rainy season branch steamers travel between the coast and Baro, at present carrying railway material. They have facilities for handling heavy cargo.

The season extends from July to September.

The Government and Niger Company's boats have no facilities for handling heavy cargo, being limited to packages capable of being handled by native labour, which is tedious and expensive.

The cost of transport by Government steamers for ordinary cargo from Forcados to Baro is from 40s. to 60s., and down from Baro to Forcados is from 21s. to 33s.

Railway Transport.—Baro to Rigachiko.

The distance is 225 miles. The railway is not yet completed to Rigachiko, where the Bauchi road starts, but I understand from railway officials that the line will be through by next March, 1911. Railhead at present is at Kogin Serikin Pawa, 172 miles from Baro, but rails are laid to within fifteen miles of Rigachiko, and this part of the line will be ready as soon as the bridges are completed.

The railway is 3 feet 6 inch gauge, and has been constructed with economy always in view. Up to the present there is no ballast on the line, and consequently there are serious delays during the rainy season owing to derailment of engines and the washout of embankments. My journey from Baro to railhead occupied fifteen days; the most of this time was lost owing to breakdowns on the line.

The journey should occupy two days, and I have no doubt that by March next it will be possible to get from Baro to Rigachiko in two days.

The freight on the line at present is 8s. per ton per mile, equal to £7 10s. per ton from Baro to Rigachiko, but at present the railway company will not undertake to transport cargo unless it is accompanied, and even then they will take no responsibility.

I understand that in the next year, when the railway is open to Zaria, the freight will be reduced to 6s. per ton per mile, equal to £5 12s. 6d. per ton from Baro to Rigachiko.

Road Transport.—Rigachiko to Naraguta.

The distance is approximately 135 miles. On my journey across by this road I took eight days, which is as quick as can be expected.

The Government engineers are clearing a track twelve feet wide, and pulling out tree stumps. They are also grading down banks of creeks to one in ten.

They are expending £20 per mile on this work, and have completed fifty miles in two months.

This road track will come into the tin fields at Toro, twelve miles north-east of Naraguta, and twelve miles west of the company's property at Federri. This track should be finished by the end of the year.

The country is flat and very easy for road building. There are four large rivers to cross, which would require bridges of over 100 feet in length, and numerous small creeks which could be bridged cheaply.

There is plenty of stone suitable for road ballast, available near the road. When the road track is through to the tin fields it will be possible to transport stores by carrier in seven days from railway.

It may be mentioned here that the Niger Company up to the present have had great difficulty with the prospectors and others travelling up to the tin fields, owing, in some cases, to their not having left themselves entirely in the hands of the company. The Niger Company have practically controlled the country, and have perfected arrangements by which they can supply large numbers of natives for carrying goods from the river to the tin field, but on several occasions their organisation has been interfered with by persons offering the natives three or four times their usual pay in order to get them through quickly to the fields. This, of course, as will be seen, is a dangerous policy, for if a scale is not strictly adhered to, the time will come when the natives will start attempting to dictate their own terms.

The Niger Company are not in favour of the motor route from the head of the Baro-Kano to the fields. Their opinion is that the money would be wasted on such a road, and that the mining community should be satisfied to wait until the railway is made. Their view is that the mining companies should join together and come to an arrangement with the Niger Company for carrying all the goods along their own route from Loko to the field *via* Keffi and Bukeru. This road, they say, could be reserved for mining business, and they would open up another route, starting from a point near Sinkai higher up the Benue River, which could be used for ordinary commercial purposes. They point out that with the rush of goods required for the mines, they have been unable to get up a sufficient and proper supply of provisions. This question, of course, requires careful consideration, as although the Niger Company wish to be considered as offering this advice in a purely disinterested manner, it should be remembered that they are asking for contracts for the whole of the transport, which would enable them to employ thousands of natives at a very low figure.

THE BAUCHI PROVINCE

Meantime the energetic prospecting and mining work that is being done in the Province of Bauchi is establishing the fact that the new tin area is of enormous extent and value both in the nature of alluvial gravels and the more permanent form of tin lodes. Mr. Lush, the well-known mining authority, who has examined a great part of the Province, estimates that these deposits are scattered over an area of no less than 2,500 square miles, and the tin produced is considered to be some of the best ever imported into Europe, and commands a price equal, if not higher, than the Straits tin. The land is situated about 3,000 to 4,000 feet above sea-level, and the late Director of Mines in Northern Nigeria states that the climate is equal to that of Rhodesia, if not even better.

"Few people have any idea," Mr. Tomson asserts, "of the possibilities of this country. It is quite a mistake to think it is unhealthy. Naraguta is over 3,500 feet above the sea-level, and is a healthy and fertile district. Here you are hundreds of miles away from the malarial swamps and the coast. If you walk up out of the town of Naraguta on to rising ground, as far as you can see stretch out great plains of waving grass, here and there dotted with masses of the Fulani cattle. It would make a splendid wheat-growing district, for the land requires very little cultivation, and there is no bush country. Kano, which lies nearly two hundred miles to the north, is a remarkable place. Several travellers have stated that it is the largest market in the world."

CLIMATE AND WATER

Mr. Huddart, until recently Director of Mines, who has declared that the climate of Northern Nigeria is better than that of Rhodesia, and that the country is without a single tsetse belt, says:

"The nights are quite cold, and any man who lives well ought to have perfect health. I do not reckon it in the least like any other part of West Africa; it is more like Eastern Soudan, and it is known as the Western Soudan. With regard to water, which, as you know, is a very important question, it is quite erroneous to imagine that there is very little water here. In Northern Queensland and South-Eastern and Western Australia there is much less water than here; in fact there is no comparison between them. Mr. Lush and I—and I had the pleasure of travelling with him—were never at any trouble in getting water, we never had even to carry water, and those who have travelled know what that means."

In Nigeria they have only two well-defined seasons, the wet and the dry season. The wet season lasts from April till the end of October, and during that time it is very difficult to do any prospecting work, although, of course, mining can be carried on in certain districts. It is during the dry season, from the end of October to April, that most of the work can be accomplished, especially from a prospector's point of view.

LIVING AND PROVISIONS

Mr. Lush, writing on the subject of the cost of living and provisions, says "living is cheap, there being plenty of beef, mutton, fowls, milk, eggs, &c. Any kind of vegetable grows well, especially English varieties; in fact very few mining fields that I have visited can be compared to Northern Nigeria in respect of the various sorts of wholesome fresh food that can be obtained. In fact all one requires is flour and a few groceries. The country will provide the rest."

LICENCES AND LEASES

The new mining regulations, incorporated in the "Minerals Proclamation, 1910," have already been published in Nigeria, but they are not yet obtainable in this country, and I am privileged to be able to reproduce a copy of them as an appendix to this book. From this document it will be seen that a prospector must either take out a prospecting right, which costs £5 per annum, and entitles the holder to explore for minerals in those parts of the Protectorate not already leased or reserved by Government notice, or an exclusive licence to prospect within an area not exceeding 16 square miles for a fee of £5 per square mile. Mining leases are only granted to holders of either one of these permits, who, upon application, must show that *bonâ fide* prospecting operations have been carried on on the area applied for, and that they possess or command sufficient working capital to ensure the proper development and working of the mine. Leases of tin areas, which are granted for a term up to twenty-one years, with the option to renew for a further twenty-one years, are three in number, viz., lode mining leases, which may be obtained up to a maximum of thirty claims of 80,000 square feet per claim, at the rental of £4 per claim per annum; alluvial mining leases, not exceeding 800 acres in area, with a minimum width throughout of 400 yards, at a rate of 5s. per acre per annum; and stream mining leases, which shall be confined to the bed of a stream, not exceeding one mile in length, at a rental of £1 per 100 yards per annum. Penalties in the shape of fines or imprisonment are to be inflicted for prospecting without a licence or working a mine without a lease, for interfering with a prospector in the exercise of his rights, for giving false information in an application for a mining lease, or for "salting" a mine, and the Government reserve the power to cancel a prospecting right or revoke a mining lease for certain breaches of the new regulations. Over and above the fees charged for yearly rental of leases, the holder is by statute required to pay a royalty of 5 per cent. to the Niger Company on the value of all metal won, and another royalty of 5 per cent. to the Government, who collect their royalty in the form of export duty.

LABOUR

A population estimated at seven to nine millions is already on the land, and although their labour would not be very efficient so far as skilled work is concerned, there is plenty of rough work to be done, for which about 6d. per day is paid. The costs of treatment are not expected to exceed 6d. per cubic yard. When it is remembered that it is possible for one property to contain many hundreds of thousands of cubic yards of alluvial wash, and that this alluvial tinstone is worth approximately 10d. per lb. at the present time, it will be realised that with the working costs at the liberal figure of 6d. per cubic yard, there is a very considerable margin of profit in these undertakings.

Mr. J. Tomson says of the natives that they make very good labourers: "They insist on being paid with English money, 'threepenny bits' being very popular. They have no liking for gold, and do not consider it so valuable as silver. The pagans, who are the farming class, appear to be a most industrious people. They still live in fear of invading Fulani, and always take their bows and arrows with them to the field. Neither men nor women wear dress of any kind. They have a juju or secret oath which forbids them to put on any garment. With these people the missionaries make no headway at all. Neither do they with the Mohammedans."

The manager of the Lucky Chance Mines, reporting under date 29th August, said he was still paying 6d. per day for ordinary labour, and so far he had had little trouble with the men on day wages, although they had several times tried to get him to raise the rate of pay.

Reporting on a property at Juga in the tin district, Mr. Huddart says:

"The properties are very favourably situated to obtain labour. The men from Bauchi and the east come along the main caravan route looking for work to enable them to earn money to pay the taxes, &c. As this particular property is near the market, and the men usually halt at the market, they can easily be recruited. The cost of ordinary labour is 1d. per hour, and is easily trained. The Bornu and Eastern Kanuri are, in my opinion, the best workers available. A further advantage lies in the position of the property in settled country under the control of the Filani Emir of Bauchi, and the men prefer this to the pagan country."

Referring to another property about twenty miles further south, Mr. Huddart says:

"When all is in proper working order, I am convinced that ample labour will be forthcoming, as the property is favourably situated in that it can tap the Angass country and the western part of Bornu, as well as the eastern Bauchi territory. When the proper camps are made, markets organised, and the natives learn that a certain income awaits them, I feel sure that labour will come in without any difficulty, and I speak as one knowing their language and having an intimate knowledge of the conditions."

Mr. H. W. Laws, General Mining Manager of the Niger Company, in his report to the Bisichi Company, whose property is near Naraguta, says:

"There is a good supply of labour in the country; owing to a sudden increase in the demand for labour a temporary shortage was reported this wet season, but the labour market is now rapidly recovering, and in view of the very large amount of labour available in the Hausa States, and the Province of Bornu, no difficulties need be anticipated as to the supply in future."

The concensus of opinions held by men who understand the amount and nature of the work entailed in this particular form of mining, and are, at the same time, personally familiar with the material that the country has to offer for the purpose, shows that the supply of labour in Northern Nigeria is entirely adequate, and although the development of West Africa depends almost entirely upon the labour question, there is no prospect of any difficulty on this account. Mr. Astley Cooper believes the chief grounds upon which trouble might arise, are the desire of the majority of the natives not to do too much work, the fear that a few months' work in the mines would give a native sufficient money to live on for a year or two, and the difficulty of getting the right sort of European to take charge of the native labourers. But after all there is little reason to anticipate trouble on any one of these counts. No native in any part of the globe does more work than he is kindly but firmly obliged to perform, and there is no necessity for employers to demoralise the native labourers by a policy of over-payment. But the necessity of employing the right sort of European to put in control over the natives is quite to the point. The West African is more domestic than the Kaffir—of whom there are over 200,000 at work in the Transvaal mines—and there is no more willing worker if he has the proper white man over him. But it is the duty of the Government and the trading companies, and the mining corporations, to select the right men for their purpose, and if they are wise in this respect there need be no fear of labour troubles in either Southern or Northern Nigeria.

THE FUTURE OF THE FIELD

The published opinions of Government officials, engineers of repute, capitalists, traders, and travellers, all tend to prove that in Northern Nigeria we have one of the largest, if not the very largest, of the tin-producing areas of the world. Other minerals are known to exist, and very big developments may be looked for in the near future, as the pioneering efforts of the Niger Company and the Champion Gold Reefs of West Africa are being followed by powerful financial houses, but alluvial tin stands out, and will always stand out, as the leading product of this remarkable mineral country.

Two such astute men and persons so well acquainted with the country as Sir Walter Egerton, the Governor of Southern Nigeria, and the late Sir Alfred Jones, have expressed the strongest views as to the extent and importance of these tin deposits, and the acting Governor of Northern Nigeria in his latest report asserted that "with the introduction of more capital and a good means of transport from the field to the railway a very large development is anticipated."

Mr. Lush says the Bauchi tin deposits are richer than he has seen in any part of the world. It is, he says, a granite country, and although the existence of reefs has been proved in one part of the district, the alluvial deposits—which yield tin oxide containing about 72 per cent. of metallic tin—are of principal importance.

ALLUVIAL AND LODE MINING

Alluvial mining, has, of course, the demerit of being short-lived. There is no great depth in the deposits, and especially if they are worked economically—that is to say rapidly—they are exhausted in a comparatively short time. But the attention directed to the district in these alluvial workings will certainly lead to the discovery and opening-up of the tin lodes, which in course of time should prove a more lasting source of supply than the alluvials. Indeed, at two points, two tin lodes are already being opened up, and before long a good idea should be obtained of their value. The interests at work in the district will certainly see that every chance is given to this side of the business, but, of course, development upon a lode is very different work to that upon alluvial deposits, and progress may be slower in their case. It is very unlikely, with such an enormous area of stanniferous gravels, that lodes of importance should not be discovered as time goes on, and there appears to be no doubt that the tin production of Nigeria will become quite a factor in the markets of the world. Many things will have to happen before lode producing can be carried out upon a large scale, but as the alluvials are worked out, the labour employed upon them can be concentrated upon the most lasting deposits, and the operations of the alluvial miners should produce a working population which should be fitted to deal with the higher form of mining. Certain facilities will doubtless be given to the district, and some idea of the importance and the developments in this part of Nigeria can be gathered from the fact that the Bank of British West Africa has been earnestly invited to open an office in Bauchi. At present this matter is under consideration, since it is difficult to fix upon a spot which will be most suitable for such an institution to work, but before long it is probable that the tin-mining district will have the facilities offered by a bank.

THE GENERAL PROSPECTS

Mr. Oliver Wethered, whose name is so well known in connection with the tin industry, has described to a meeting of shareholders the peculiar advantages of the country which is now attracting the attention of the tin markets of the world, and in the course of his address he said:

"Now as to the country in which our interests are centred, judging by the information that I have received from all available quarters, I have no hesitation in stating that we are interested in one of the most important virgin alluvial tin fields the world has ever seen, and certainly the most important that capitalists have had an opportunity of working as a new field. In Tasmania, Australia, and other countries which have produced large quantities of alluvial tin, the prospectors have gone in by hundreds, and even thousands, and have washed out large quantities of tin greatly to their own individual benefit. Subsequently the ground has been worked over and over again, and in recent years again re-worked by means of modern appliances. I may say here, that in Cornwall some of the ground must have been worked eight or ten times, and big plants are now being erected for the purpose of working it again by modern methods. It will be obvious to every one that with a practically untouched field, and working in the most economical and thorough way from the start, the results cannot fail to be extremely satisfactory.

"Undoubtedly one of the factors which has delayed the opening up of the tin fields of Nigeria has been the question of economical transport. But the Nigeria tin is of very high quality. It fetches, as a rule, anywhere from £6 to £8 more a ton than Cornish tin, and in this connection I should like to read an extract from a letter which was written to me by the managing director of the largest tin smelting works in Europe, to whom I sent a sample of the tin oxide as it was received here, and of which, in acknowledging it, he says, 'It is about 75 per cent. metallic tin, of excellent quality, equal to anything being put on the market, so far as my observation goes.' I am very closely connected with Cornish mining, and there we get Bolivian, Straits, and all kinds of tin, and it is the general opinion that Nigerian tin is one of the very best tins imported into Europe, and will always command a price equal to, if not better than, that of the Straits. Even under existing conditions alluvial tin mining in Nigeria is a highly profitable business, but when the present railway system is completed, and the road made from the Government line to the tin field, the freight should be reduced by many pounds per ton, and the profit largely increased. The completion of the road would enable heavy machinery to be brought to the mines, when larger quantities of the rich alluvial ground would be handled in an economical way, and the work done at a cost much below what is possible under existing conditions. The lodes, too, of which there is undoubted evidence, could be worked. Meanwhile some machinery can be transported in sections, and the output of tin should be rapidly increased and the costs greatly reduced."

Mr. Assheton Lever, in summing up the situation generally in Northern Nigeria to a meeting of shareholders, said:

"We know that there are considerable areas there which in some cases are very rich in alluvial tin. There are also tin lodes there; but that for the present is another story, because alluvial tin is a thing which is easily and comparatively inexpensively worked, whereas to work a lode mine requires good means of transport, and to be able to get up to the mines easily expensive and heavy machinery. We have a good climate, we have a sufficiency of water, and so far as we can ascertain, we have a sufficiency of native labour. All the companies which are interested in Northern Nigeria appear anxious to co-operate, and are willing to work together generally for their mutual benefit, and for the tin industry in particular."

Mr. H. W. Lake, the consulting engineer, speaking in a professional capacity at the same meeting, referred to the phenomenal richness of the river banks in the tin district in Northern Nigeria, while very rich alluvials are found on the flats, and when it comes to investigation of the river banks themselves very much larger quantities of black tin to the cubic yard are won. "I am speaking now," he added, "from a certain amount of experience, because four years ago we had an expedition in the Bauchi district, and our engineer obtained some quite remarkable results from the alluvial. Of course, it is a new country. There is a great deal of pioneering work to be done, and what we have still to look forward to is steady systematic organisation for the next year or two. We do not want to make the mistakes that have been made in the opening up of many new countries—some of them not very far from Nigeria—but we do want to settle down to steady systematic development. As far as the railway is concerned, there seems no doubt that we shall have a line into the tin fields, which is going to simplify the question of transport, and reduce the costs very materially. With regard to the actual working of these alluvials, to begin with, I am of opinion that we should use the simplest methods possible—ground sluicing and so forth, but there will come a time when we shall have very seriously to consider the question of hydraulicing and treating these alluvials on a very much larger scale than would be possible by means of sluicing."

A DISTRICT FULL OF NARAGUTAS

The extraordinary results obtained by the Naraguta Company might be regarded as exceptional, since it was a proved mine when taken over from the Niger Company, and the actual work done upon it has only confirmed what was previously known of its phenomenal value. But it may be said with great confidence, after careful examination, by not one, but many engineers, that the picture is not in any degree overdrawn. Moreover, the head of a great firm of mining engineers who was inclined to ridicule the values reported, has since admitted that he has altogether changed his opinion, and that he thinks from advices he has received, that the Malay Peninsula fields, even in their palmiest days, were never "in it" with the Northern Nigerian alluvial tin fields. In one place tin has been taken out, on the Dubbo property, belonging to the Lucky Chance Mines, extending over 640 acres, which actually goes 120 lbs. to the cubic yard. That is to say, that the calabashers must be getting out tin almost pure. This may be only a pocket; but the whole character of the reports from the fields makes it perfectly certain that the general nature of the Bauchi district, where the alluvial tin is mostly found, is of an absolutely phenomenal character.

There is no doubt whatever that in this remote district of Nigeria, which until a few years ago, was closed to the white man by the ferocity of its inhabitants, nature has been concentrating tin for thousands and tens of thousands of years, until we have it now in very large quantities in an almost pure condition. To Sir Percy Girouard is largely due the honour of opening up this country, through the discipline he and his subordinates dealt out to the original inhabitants. To his successor, Sir Hesketh Bell, fell the duty and the honour of opening up further the country by a railway system which will make it a great Imperial acquisition.

The work of Sir Percy Girouard and Sir Hesketh Bell may be specially referred to, for they represent the Imperial Government; but we must not forget the work of the directors of the pioneer companies in London, who must have worked continually to do what they have done. In the short space of only twelve months they have accomplished an amount of work which ordinary directors without enthusiasm would have taken years to do. The country has been searched for good properties, engineers have been despatched and machinery ordered, and such is the good work done in a small way with high values, that it is no exaggeration to say that many properties are now paying their way. All has been so swiftly done, and with so little fuss, that it seems like a fairy tale, and the public have no conception yet of the extraordinary value of these alluvial tin propositions in Northern Nigeria.

POLITICAL AND COMMERCIAL OUTLOOK

It is satisfactory to gather from the report of the acting Governor dated 11th December last, that the year 1909 was a very peaceful one, the military operations which it was found necessary to carry out being on a small scale, and chiefly on account of highway robberies. From all the Provinces it is reported that the general feeling of the Emirs and native chiefs towards the

British Administration continues to be most friendly. They are beginning to show an intelligent interest and zeal in the political work, and political officers are receiving support in any scheme proposed for the improvement of the Native Administration. The people show signs of wishing to be on friendly terms with the Government, and the agricultural classes are feeling a sense of security which enables them to spread out in all directions and take up new holdings. Their present position is described as "one of progressive tranquillity and content." The inter-colonial traffic in slaves has already ceased; local slave-dealing is not entirely stamped out, but it is not extensive, and last year 1,392 slaves were freed, practically all by means of native courts, the majority of these ex-slaves being self-redeemed.

The cultivation of food stuffs has increased; new markets have been established, and the present safety of the roads has greatly stimulated the internal trade of the country. A great improvement in the export trade has followed the extension of the Baro-Kano Railway. To the north of Minna there is a most extensive area of shea butter trees, but very little of the produce of this area has so far been placed on the market, partly on account of the cost of transport, and partly owing to the reluctance of the pagans to have intercourse with markets outside their districts. The construction of the railway has done much towards gaining the confidence of these people, and the reduction in the cost of transport, consequent upon the completion of the railway, will render it possible to place profitably this sylvan produce on European markets. Further north the railway will pass through the rich agricultural and stock-raising Lausa provinces, which at present export live-stock, skins, and potass by means of annual caravans. The idea that Northern Nigeria is an especially unhealthy place for European residents is scarcely borne out by the total death-rate of roughly twenty per thousand, calculated on the average resident European population; but the proportion of officers invalided home is still large, though it is much smaller than it was a few years ago, when less satisfactory sanitary conditions prevailed at the stations.

Although the addition of the Nigerian Protectorates to the Empire is primarily due to the prescience and enterprise of the Niger Company, that corporation has no monopoly of trade within their boundaries nor any special advantage over other traders. It takes its chances against rival firms in the many spots in which it comes into competition with them. At Gana Gana, for instance, the company's first station beyond Burutu, the German firm of Bey & Zimmer has a depôt. John Holt & Co., E. H. Stern & Co., J. T. Palmer & Co., Pagenstecher, and the British Cotton Growing Association are all represented in Nigeria, and the firm of G. W. Christian & Co. has established important trading stations at most of the principal towns on the river. As recently as 1904 Messrs. Christian started operations in Nigeria at a small place named Proropro on the left bank of the Niger; to-day they have branches at Forcados, Burutu, Onitsha, Illah, Illushi, Idah, and Lokoja, and at all these centres they not only conduct a large cash and barter trade, but undertake equipments and accept commissions, and cater in every way for the require- ments of both Europeans and natives. The extraordinarily rapid rise and progress of this firm is almost entirely due to the excep- tional qualifications for the trade possessed by the principal, Mr. George William Christian, who was born in Liverpool in 1872, and who, from the early age of fifteen has been associated with West Africa, and in twenty-five years has acquired a thorough experience and first-hand knowledge of the British and native needs of the Protectorates.

PARTICULARS OF COMPANIES WORKING TIN PROPERTIES IN NORTHERN NIGERIA

CHAMPION GOLD REEFS OF WEST AFRICA, Ltd.

Capital.—£50,000, in 200,000 shares of 5s. each; all are issued and fully paid.

Directors.—S. R. Bastard (Chairman), F. N. Best, Sir Horace C. Regnart, John Waddington.

Secretary.—Newman Ogle.

Offices.—Friars House, New Broad Street, E.C.

To this company belongs the credit of being one of the first to appreciate the almost unlimited opportunities the tin fields of Northern Nigeria offer for the employment of British capital. It is not surprising, therefore, that it has to-day, not merely one finger, but the whole of its digits in the Nigerian "pie," from which it has already pulled out a "plum" in the shape of a dividend of 100 per cent. paid in March last. It is not always the pioneer in a new mining field who strikes the richest areas, but under the guidance of its highly capable engineers, Champion Gold Reefs of West Africa obtained exclusive rights over some properties and interests in options over others which promise a magnificent harvest in years to come.

It was in September 1909, that the company decided to abandon gold mining in Ashanti and devote attention to tin mining in Northern Nigeria. What were described as "very extensive alluvial tin areas" were acquired on September 20. In a circular to the shareholders, dated October 6, it was stated that the work carried on by the Niger Company, and the investigations of mining engineers in the district had "proved the existence of very rich alluvial ground, and already upwards of 1,000 tons of black tin, won by means of calabashes and sluice boxes, had been shipped." It was further stated that on one of the properties, over which the company had exclusive rights, there was a waterfall of 480 feet, which would secure cheap and ample power; that the properties were situated some 3,500 feet above sea-level, and the climate was good; that the district was thickly populated, and the natives willing and anxious to work.

The first members of the staff sailed for Northern Nigeria on October 6, and were followed a month later by Mr. Charles G. Lush, the well-known expert on the working of alluvial tin deposits. Mr. Lush was to advise as to the best method of developing the company's property, which was then stated to be 13 square miles in extent. Parenthetically it may be mentioned that other suitable areas were afterwards taken up and several handed over to subsidiary concerns. Mr. Lush first went to the Juga and Sub-Juga properties, and the first communication received from him was the following cable, dated Bauchi, December 17: "Have visited Juga, am very favourably impressed. Up to the present time proved alluvial extends over 200 acres and averages 9 feet; alluvial contains 4s. per cubic yard; the value of stream tin, £600,000. I will visit Sub-Juga this week." On December 22 he again cabled as follows: "Sub-Juga—Have visited, am very favourably impressed. I consider admirably adapted for the

Australian method of working. It will be necessary to erect a dam; will make survey and report upon. Alluvial extends over 500 acres and averages 9 feet. Estimated value of stream tin, 2s. 6d. per cubic yard." From these and other communications subsequently received it was evident that Mr. Lush had been most favourably impressed with the field generally, and with the value of the Champion Gold Reefs property in particular.

Four subsidiary companies have been formed to date, viz.:

Naraguta (Nigeria) Tin Mines, Ltd.

Lucky Chance Mines, Ltd.

Juga (Nigeria) Tin and Power Company, Ltd.

Tin Fields of Northern Nigeria, Ltd.

The Naraguta (Nigeria) Tin Mines is not only a productive concern, but one that has already entered the dividend list, 1s. per share having been distributed. The property was originally five square miles in extent, but the area has since been extended. It was held under option by Champion Gold Reefs, who transferred their option to the present company. The purchase consideration paid to the Niger Company was £50,000, payable as to £30,000 in cash and £20,000 in fully-paid shares. The Government and the Niger Company are together entitled to a royalty of 10 per cent. on the profits. Before the present company was formed the Niger Company obtained from the Naraguta property over 1,000 tons of tin concentrates, and it is stated that in one square mile of the property, which has been systematically tested by pits, there are 10,000 tons of black tin awaiting extraction. Up to the present time, the ground treated has produced tin to the value of £3,000 per acre, whereas in other countries, such as Australia and the Malay Peninsula, £1,000 per acre is considered phenomenal. Some of the ground gives fully 5 lbs. of tin to the cubic yard. There can be no doubt that Naraguta is going to be one of the "gems" of the district.

The Lucky Chance Mines, Ltd., was originally formed in May, 1905, to acquire property in New Zealand, but at the end of 1908 only seven shares had been issued, and the paid-up capital was £5 5s., the company having no assets or liabilities. Towards the end of last year, however, it was placed on its financial legs by the Champion Gold Reefs of West Africa. The latter company sold certain of its tin areas to the Lucky Chance Company for 200,000 shares, and agreed to procure the subscription of 8,000 further shares. To-day the Lucky Chance Company is a robust and ably-controlled enterprise, with excellent prospects of development. Its properties comprise nearly 12,000 acres. The South Juga property has recently been sold to the Juga (Nigeria) Tin and Power Company for £10,000.

The Juga (Nigeria) Tin and Power Company owns what is known as the Juga property, which is situated on a plateau 3,280 feet above sea-level, having a total area of 1,600 acres, and the Sub-Juga property, which lies upon the lower plateau immediately below Juga, the area in this case being 6,720 acres. As already remarked, the South Juga property has recently been added. Mr. Lush estimates that 200 acres of the Juga property will be highly payable. For the purposes of his estimate, he took the average depth as 9 feet, which, extending over 200 acres, equals 2,904,000 cubic yards, each cubic yard containing 6 lbs. "In valuing the ground at 6 lbs. per cubic yard," Mr. Lush said, "I am not taking into account only the high results obtained from some of the bottom wash, but am reckoning it as a whole. I do this because working results may prove that the wash does not extend over the whole 200 acres, but the gravel does, and I feel confident will average what I state." In a similar way he estimated that the Sub-Juga property would yield 3 lbs. per cubic yard over 5,808,000 cubic yards.

Tin Fields of Northern Nigeria, Ltd., is a company owning eight square miles at Federri and nine square miles near Dila River, both in the Bauchi Province.

In addition to having floated these companies—in which, of course, Champion Gold Reefs retains a large interest—the company has also large holdings in the following concerns:

Northern Nigeria (Bauchi) Tin Mines.

Anglo-Continental Mines, Ltd.

Anchor Diamond Mines.

It also still owns a lease over five square miles in Ashanti.

NARAGUTA (NIGERIA) TIN MINES, Ltd.

Capital.—£175,000, divided into 175,000 shares of £1 each, of which 158,500 are issued and fully paid.

Directors.—Frank N. Best (Chairman), H. C. Godfray, Herbert Moir, John Waddington, H. Bousquet, H. S. Reitlinger.

Secretary.—Newman Ogle.

Offices.—Friars House, New Broad Street, E.C.

This company owns an area of 3,200 acres at Naraguta, and two further blocks known as the "C" and "Q" areas of eight square miles. It was formerly worked by the Niger Company, who won from the alluvial beds its 1,000 tons of tin concentrates.

The company was registered on 15th January, and the property was taken over on 4th February. Mr. C. G. Lush, the company's consulting engineer, has inspected the property, and has stated that on the Naraguta property they had ground which would give fully 5 lbs. of tin to the cubic yard. He further reported that ten acres had already been treated and given that result, which could be taken as a very fair prospecting whole.

The returns up to and including the month of October 1910 amounted to a total of 350 tons of tin oxide made up as follows:

1910	Tons
February	28
March	34
April	36
May	36
June	37
July	44
August	45
September	45
October	45
	350

Good profits can be, and are being, made under the present primitive methods in use, but the greatly increased profits to which the management is looking forward can only be secured by adopting the most up-to-date machinery, such as is used in Tasmania and other countries. In order to assure success experienced men are being brought from Tasmania by the Champion Gold Reefs group, and the Naraguta Company will have the benefit of their advice.

At the statutory meeting in April last the chairman stated: "We have the proud distinction of owning the property from which the first shipments of tin were made—not only that, but one of the richest out there, and I am quite confident this company can look forward to a very successful career. The extent of our property is four square miles, one mile only of which has been thoroughly prospected, and calculated to contain 10,000 tons of tin oxide. At the present market price of tin this should yield over £500,000 profit. Our engineer tells me that up to the present time every acre of ground so far treated has produced tin to the value of £3,000, whereas in other countries, such as Australia and Malay, £1,000 per acre is considered phenomenal: therefore, I consider we can congratulate ourselves upon being interested in such a unique proposition."

As an indication of what may be expected when improved working methods have been introduced, Mr. C. G. Lush states that thirty men and one plant will be able to produce as much and even more tin than is now being obtained with three hundred men. "If we put only one plant on the property," he says, "it will take us, perhaps, a hundred years to work it out, but there is no reason why we should not have four or five plants, and work it out in a lifetime!" In Australia, Tasmania, and the Straits Settlements 1½ lbs. of tin per cubic yard is considered very good, but Mr. Lush is of opinion that in Naraguta the ground will give fully 5 lbs. of tin per cubic yard; in fact, 10 acres have already been treated, and have given that result, which can be taken as "a very fair prospecting whole." All that is necessary is to get the plant there as soon as possible.

In Mr. Frank D. Bourke the company has an excellent and indefatigable manager, and recently the directors engaged the services of Mr. A. F. Kitto, who left on October 12 to assist Mr. Bourke in the management.

LUCKY CHANCE MINES, Ltd.

Capital.—£75,000 in 300,000 shares of 5s. each, all issued and fully paid.

Directors.—Mr. S. R. Bastard (Chairman), Mr. F. N. Best, and Mr. Oliver Wethered.

Secretary.—Mr. Newman Ogle.

Offices.—Friars House, New Broad Street, E.C.

This company owns the following properties:—

(1) *Dubbo.*—A property in Bauchi, Northern Nigeria, consisting of 632 acres. This property is under the charge of two engineers.

(2) *Rafinsiroma.*—This is a small rich property of 33 acres adjoining Dubbo to the south, and capable of immediately producing tin by ground sluicing and calabashing.

(3) *Bengalili.*—A property of about 320 acres on the river Bukeru, situated about one mile to the north of Dubbo, and capable of producing tin by handworking at once.

(4) *Bengalili North.*—This is an area of about 120 acres adjoining and to the north of the Bengalili property, also capable of producing tin by sluicing and calabashing. The river runs through this property.

(5) *Polchi.*—A property of 84 acres adjoining South Juga, and situated on the main road from Toro to Bauchi. The property is now being worked and is producing tin.

(6) *Boidun.*—This property is situated on the road from Dubbo to Bri, and is about one mile west of Dubbo. It extends for a distance of about a mile along the river.

(7) *Bilidi River.*—Three square miles, or 1,920 acres. Good tin was found on this property, besides an appreciable amount of gold in the wash.

(8) *Kurdum.*—Five square miles, or 3,200 acres. On the tests made the overburden went 3 lbs. of tin for 7 feet, and the bottom wash went 60 lbs. of tin for 1 foot.

(9) *Kwall Falls.*—The first application was made on behalf of this company for this power, which would be of great value, as it gives 2,000 horse-power in the dry season, and commands several properties.

The *Dubbo* property is situated near the village of Dubbo, on the Dubbo River, and west of the Soli Hills. It is sometimes described as Topaz Valley, so named on account of the large quantity of topaz found in the wash. It is situated about six miles north of Juga. The Lireui natives have done a lot of work on this property, sinking shafts in some cases a hundred yards back from the Dubbo River. These shafts run from 8 to 10 feet in depth, proving that the bottom wash must have been very rich for, as a rule, the Lireuis only mined shallow ground where the wash is easily got. Mr. Lush said that he had not seen similar work in any other part of the tin district.

Mr. Lush reported that the pannings from the river bed gave very high values, and four shafts sunk to a depth of 8 feet averaged 6 lbs. of tin to the cubic yard. One shaft, which bottomed at 5 feet, went 30 lbs. of tin to the cubic yard. An open-cut on the river bank exposed 17 feet of gravel, which went 6 lbs. to the cubic yard. The overburden thrown out at the shafts sunk by the Lireuis, where tried, gave an average of 5 lbs. of tin to the cubic yard. At the southern end of this property Mr. Lush says the river comes down from a hill with a fall of some 350 feet through a rocky gorge. By working a dam at the top of the rapids sufficient water could be conserved to run a plant by electrical transmission. This country is mostly granite sand, no stiff clay or pug. Mr. Lush states that nearly the whole of the 632 acres are an alluvial deposit, and in his estimates, in order to be well within the mark, he estimates that the payable dirt extends over 300 acres and averages 6 feet in depth. The manager reported on August 29 that he had 300 men employed, and for the four weeks ending August 27 he had recovered 31½ tons of tin, and had cut 735 feet of water leads.

Rafinsiroma adjoins Dubbo to the south, and the manager, reporting on August 29, said he had just started work on this property. On September 4 the manager reported that he had already shipped 505 lbs., and a cablegram received October 9 states that a further shipment is being made.

Work has been started on Polchi, and on October 9 a cablegram was received stating that the first shipment had been made.

On the *Bilidi River* property Mr. Lush reported that he made several tests from wash exposed on the river bank below the Kofai crossing, and obtained payable tin results in all. He then followed up the river for about three miles, and in one part he says he got gold as well as tin in the concentrates. In five pannings he reports there were from six to ten colours of gold in every dish, which in his opinion was highly satisfactory. Two miles below the Kofai crossing he found some very promising flats, where he also got eight colours of gold in one dish. At the time of his visit he says there was sufficient water running in the Bauchi River for centrifugal pump work.

As regards *Kurdum* and *Dila Rivers*, at the lower end of the ground, near the village of Bundas, Mr. Lush says he obtained very good prospects of tin in gravel from the river bed. At Dawka, some eight miles upstream, the wash taken out of the river went 80 lbs. to the cubic yard. Several pits were sunk on the banks, but owing to soakage water only one bottomed, the depth of which was 8 feet, and gave the following result:

Overburden 7 feet went 3 lbs. of tin to the cubic yard.

Bottom wash 1 foot went 60 lbs. of tin to the cubic yard.

The river between Dawka and Bundas falls 400 feet, and at the latter town it is 30 feet by 2 feet deep, flowing at the rate of 60 feet per minute. Even in the middle of the dry season Mr. Lush says a race cut from a point about a mile upstream would give sufficient head to generate 500 h.p. by electricity.

Mr. L. H. L. Huddart, in his report on the Kurdum River concession, says he feels justified in making a preliminary estimate in order to give an idea of what the property may be proved to contain, and he bases it on the following reasons:—

(*a*) The tin falls above the property.

(*b*) The river has its source in a country rich in tin.

(*c*) The good values obtained in the stream bed and samples taken from the banks.

(*d*) The method of deposition of the alluvial which indicates that "wash outs" are unlikely to be found. In fact some good leads should have been left by the river in the older gravels.

Upon these grounds he is of opinion that there are about 300 acres of alluvial ground that should prove to be about 2½ yards deep with values of about 3 lbs. per cubic yard. Mr. Huddart adds that an output of about 30 tons per month, or 360 tons per year, should be reached without difficulty. In conclusion, he says: "The property is a good one, and its ample supply of water cannot be too strongly emphasised. Tin will be produced quickly from the river bed, and systematic development should bear out the above estimate, and enable the work to be laid out with a view on ultimate production of about 40 tons per month."

Application for the Kwall Falls for electric power has been made on behalf of this company, and great importance is attached to them. They are situated about 14 miles west of the Niger (Bauchi) Syndicate's area, and it is stated that in the driest months there is ample water flowing with a drop of 400 feet to generate 2,000 h.p. without any expense of damming.

TIN FIELDS OF NORTHERN NIGERIA, Ltd.

Capital.—£100,000 in 100,000 shares of £1 each, of which 45,000 were issued to the vendors and 24,507 for cash, 10s. paid.

Directors.—Mr. S. R. Bastard (Chairman), Mr. F. N. Best, and Mr. C. H. Dudley Ward.

Secretary.—Mr. Newman Ogle.

Offices.—Friars House, New Broad Street, E.C.

This company owns alluvial tin property at Federri comprising an area of 5,120 acres, and a further property situated on the Dila River or Doss, comprising an area of 5,760 acres.

On the Federri property a tin-bearing area of 300 acres has

been proved containing tin alluvial from 2½ to 3½ yards deep, going from 3 lbs. to 6 lbs. per cubic yard, and it is estimated that the property has a life of twenty-six years.

The second property is the Dila River or Doss, which has a proved area of tin alluvial deposit from 3 to 5 yards deep over 400 acres, with an average value of 3 lbs. per cubic yard. The life of the property has been estimated at twenty-three years. A fully qualified engineer is now in charge of the properties, and production of tin is expected to commence immediately. The consulting engineer is Mr. C. G. Lush.

JUGA (NIGERIA) TIN AND POWER COMPANY, Ltd.

Capital.—£275,000, in 275,000 £1 shares, of which all are issued.

Directors.—Sir J. West Ridgeway (Chairman), Mr. Segar Richard Bastard, Mr. Frank Norman Best, Sir Horace G. Regnart, J.P., and Mr. Henry S. Reitlinger.

Secretary.—Mr. Newman Ogle.

Offices.—Friars House, New Broad Street, E.C.

This company owns three properties, as follows:—

	Acres
(1) Juga	1600
(2) Sub-Juga	6720
(3) South Juga	1280

South Juga.—Mr. C. G. Lush, in reporting on the South Juga property, said: "On the northern end there are several native workings, in which payable prospects can be got. It would be advisable to have shafts sunk right along the lead from the Juga boundary to the Bauchi road, and boring plant used if water hindered sinking to bed-rock.... Some of the tin carried into Juga must have found its way into South Juga." Mr. L. H. L. Huddart, reporting on the property, said: "The elevation is about 3,000 feet above the sea-level, with precipitous granite hills rising at least 1,500 feet above the valley on both sides.... The tin occurs in a valley about four miles long, running north-east and south-west. Bed-rock is granite with frequent outcrops of granite and granulite, which form baths more or less at right angles to the valley. The average width is about 2,000 feet.... The ground is friable and easy to work.... A water course which rises on Juga runs right down to the valley. From December to April there is practically no running water, but from May to November the stream runs freely.... If the small tributaries are dammed, and skill is used in saving the water, there should be sufficient for all purposes for six or seven months in the year. Later on a portable pump elevating plant would have sufficient water for at least nine months. There is a considerable quantity of water held up between the granite baths, and the water-locked ground provides natural reservoirs.... A thorough system of prospecting should be inaugurated.... Pits should be put in right across the valley at 100 feet intervals, and a property plan made out showing the depth of ground valued. These will enable the mining work to be laid out in a systematic manner, and will disclose the rich leads." Mr. Huddart has formed a favourable opinion of the property, and gives the following reasons for the estimates he has prepared: (1) Amount of work previously done by natives who never touch anything but rich wash; (2) sampling and inspection of native working and their tailings; (3) the fact that this proposition is geographically a part of Juga on which rich wash exists; (4) personal knowledge of the ground tested and discoveries on every known part of this field, and general occurrence of cassiterite on all parts of the property. Taking the property as a whole, he estimates that there are 180 acres of alluvial ground, running 4 lbs. per cubic yard, averaging two yards deep. In conclusion, Mr. Huddart says this is an attractive property.... Importance is readily attached to the fact that the property can be made an immediate producer.

Juga Property.—This property is on a plateau 3,280 feet above the sea-level, and Mr. Lush estimates that 200 acres will be highly payable. He takes the average depth of ground as 9 feet, and this extending for 200 acres equals 2,904,000 cubic yards. The area is of exceedingly high quality, and exceptionally free from impurities. In his report Mr. Lush says: "Valuing the ground at 6 lbs. per cubic yard, I am not taking into account only the high results obtained from some of the bottom wash, but am reckoning it as a whole. I do this because working results may prove that the wash does not extend over the whole 200 acres, but the gravel does, and I feel confident will average what I state."

Sub-Juga.—This property, comprising an area of 6,720 acres, lies upon the lower plateau, or plain, immediately below Juga. The natives have done a great deal of work here, and their beds were extensively tried by Mr. Lush, who got very rich prospects when panning. Some of the dish concentrates went as high as 40 lbs. of tin oxide to the cubic yard, and in no single instance did he get less than 3 lbs. He considers that out of the 6,720 acres 400 are proved to be highly payable, but this only includes the main lead, which runs right through the property for 6¼ miles, and does not include any of the runs coming in from east and west. He takes the average depth of ground as 9 feet; this extending for 400 acres equals 5,808,000 cubic yards. Mr. Lush has recommended movable plants for these properties. Transmission of electrical power to run both the nozzle and the gravel pumps is, of course, the cheapest and best method of working, but it will be some time, probably two years, before the contemplated hydraulical scheme can be installed. Mr. Lush's recommendations have been accepted by the board, and two plants are being constructed, and their cost when mounted and erected at the mine will not exceed £10,000. In addition to the sluice boxes at present on the property, there are now on the way a further sixty-nine sluice boxes, with all exhausters complete, and these will enable sluicing and calabashing to be carried on pending the arrival and erection of the hydraulic plant.

Mr. Hooke has been appointed manager, with Mr. Grant as his assistant. Besides sluicing, surveys have to be completed, dams constructed, prospecting done, especially by means of boring, tools being supplied for those parts where the water is too heavy for the pits to be sunk.

Mr. A. W. Hooke writes under date September 14, 1910, as follows:

"Attached hereto are my notes upon the leases of the company and the dam site. In setting forth this general report several diffi-culties have faced the writer—the absence of any systematic sampling record—the flooded condition of the existing holes, and the short time in which to cover the ground.

"At the same time also an effort had to be made to organise the labour and increase the output under existing circumstances. I give the following summary to show how the output has increased in the last four weeks. From August 15 to September 10 the production stands thus:

Week ending.		Calabashers.	Crude Tin Won.	Purchased at	
August	20	52 men	768 lbs.	¾d.	per lb.
”	27	102 ”	3,319 ”	¾d.	”
Sept.	3	127 ”	3,327 ”	¾d.	”
”	10	133 ”	4,925 ”	½d.	”

"Some of this ore is being won on Juga, but by far the greater part comes from Nafuta. It contains much iron impurity, and a streaming box has already been made for its re-treatment at Juga. It will be understood that the natives bring their weekly winnings from Nafuta to Juga on Sundays, when it is weighed and purchased from them. The first three lots shown above were purchased approximately at ¾d. per lb., and the last one at ½d. The condition of the tin, &c., is a big factor in guiding one as to the price, but as time goes on I hope to instruct the native into the way of streaming his tin and bringing it to a better quality. If I can do this, and keep the price down, it means a big advantage to us.

"Labour at 6d. per day is most satisfactory (9d. is the ruling rate elsewhere except at Dubbo). This week my whole gang struck work and demanded an increase from 6d. to 9d. I flatly refused, and to time of writing have almost as many new men as I require. Some of the old hands have since returned to work. I have despatched a headman to Gingim and Polchi, who will doubtless secure all that I require.

"At Nafuta sampling shafts are being sunk at the rate of about nine per week. These cannot be quite bottomed on account of the water in the wash, but as the rain eases off they can be completed and sampled.

"*General.*—The three leases are all properties upon which hydraulic sluicing can be carried out satisfactorily, and the wash and overburden in each case is ideal material for gravel pumping. I am quite pleased with the general condition of things, but am anxious to have my sampling completed, so that I may form some estimate of yardage and the average value."

PRELIMINARY REPORT BY MR. ARTHUR W. HOOKE, ACCOMPANYING HIS LETTER OF SEPTEMBER 14, 1910.

Juga Property.—This lease stands at the highest elevation of the three, and practically forms the divide between South Juga and Nafuta. Its watershed is large, and the greater portion of this goes north-east through the Nafuta gorge to the flats. The lease embraces an area of 1,440 acres and compasses the flats adjacent to two streams coming from the South, which unite and continue north-east, passing into the Nafuta gorge as the Juga River.

The maximum depth of the ground is only about 12 feet, and much of it is amenable to ground sluicing, though it could be handled more advantageously by gravel pumps. This latter scheme is eventually the policy to adopt, as thereby most of the material can be stacked after treatment, and any chance of silting-up be avoided.

The former (ground sluicing) will be a temporary expedient—I say temporary advisedly, because the detritus from such operations will eventually find its way to the area for the dam site above the Nafuta gorge. It will be readily understood that the shape of the property is irregular in order to most economically take in the desired area.

The rocky surroundings naturally bring down their storm waters rapidly, and this will always act as a deterrent in ground sluicing and be a point in favour of power plants.

The lease carries a sparse supply of timber, but will justify the installation of a steam plant of such dimensions as that already under construction. As time wears on, however, an alternative power must have consideration.

The contour of the country does not lend itself to the construction of earthwork headraces, &c., being too rocky; service water, will therefore have to be carried in a pipe service.

I am forwarding a sketch plan showing the two streams and their confluence under the name of the Juga. Pits as shown have been sunk and a sampling done. The samples (Mr. Robinson informs me) were taken by a native headman, and run very erratically from 17 lbs. to nil per cubic yard. Robinson says that some of the holes at that time had been flooded, and is of opinion that all the bottom wash in some instances was not included in the samples taken.

At the present time all the pits are more or less flooded and silted, but I will re-sample the whole of these and advise results at the earliest possible moment.

The two dams shown in the sketch have been carried away by floods. Higher up the river at "A," a much better site exists, which will give more pressure and command more ground. I propose to place one here as soon as I can.

The tracts shown on the drawing will give some idea of the direction in which the other leases lie.

Viewed in conjunction with the plans, the directors will have a more concise idea of their relative positions.

Nafuta or Sub-Juga.—Of the exclusive area held here some 1,850 acres have been embodied in the mining lease just issued. It embraces what appears to be the pick of the Nafuta flats and encloses a maximum of alluvial drift with a minimum of rock, and at the same time adheres to the water-course. The Nafuta gorge terminates quite abruptly, and opens in an expansive plain lying some 400 feet below. The lease commences at the foot of the gorge, and runs along the river in a north-easterly direction. Its width embraces the deepest of the flats, though there is still some ground at the south-west corner of the exclusive area that warrants attention. I should say from a cursory examination that the amount of workable ground is in excess of that of the other leases, though no attempt can be made to quote tonnage until many more pits have been sunk. It is from this area that most of our present tin is being won. The tin contains much impurity, such as iron, and the natives find a difficulty in separating it by calabashing.

The average depth, judging by the present trial pits, is 12 feet. The wash is clear and medium sized, and the overburden is ideal material for removal where viewed in the old paddocks.

I see no difficulties in it as a gravel sluicing proposition, once provision is made for power. The lease carries no timber, and is a power consideration from the beginning.

Of tin value I can quote last week's winning of 4,000 odd lbs. of crude tin by 120 men with calabashes, and this too in the face of many weather difficulties.

A site has been set aside for a native village, and already people are congregating and erecting their grass huts.

South Juga.—This lease, as its name implies, lies south of Juga. It covers 855 acres, and is approximately 4 miles long by 2,000 yards wide. It is traversed for its entire length by the track which leaves the Toro-Bauchi road and comes on to Juga. The lease is narrow—it lies in a long gully, and appears bound by a succession of rocky bars. These no doubt may be acting as excellent natural tin savers, but they will make work very irregular. Of the tin value here I cannot speak with any definiteness. I have not traversed the ground in detail, and as no pits have been sunk upon it, I have no samples to guide me. It will have my attention so soon as I can get one lease into a regular producing stage.

Nafuta Dam Site.—In proceeding from Juga to Nafuta one traverses the basin of this proposed dam. As a site its position would be hard to beat. It covers some 356 acres, which narrows down to a steep rocky neck, through which the waters debouch on to the Nafuta flat. The sides of the gorge rise in an abrupt slope, and are composed of granite. It forms an ideal situation for a retaining wall which, if reared 100 feet, would throw back 326 million cubic feet of water. This quantity of water would develop approximately 550 horse-power for 370 days of 12 hours, using 1,220,000 cubic feet per day, and allowing 525,000 cubic feet for daily evaporation and soakage losses.

At present the dam area is enclosed in the Nafuta *exclusive area*, which expires at Christmas. I propose therefore to take it up as an agricultural lease, which I believe can be secured at annual rental of 1s. per acre.

The dam is a necessity for the operation of Nafuta, though, of course once established, it could generate high tension electricity for transmission to Juga and South Juga, and operate them as well.

A masonry retaining wall could, I think, be most cheaply built, as the stone exists on the site. It would be the installation of a quarrying plant of say half-dozen rock drills and channelling machines, also a small aerial line up the bed of the dam for handling the stone, and a "flying fox" gear across the gorge for handling all the stone in the retaining wall.

In some places at the lower end the water is lost to sight 30 feet or more beneath the huge granite boulders that lie in the gorge.

GONGOLA SYNDICATE, Ltd.

Capital Authorised.—£9000. Issued and fully paid, £6607.

Directors.—Mr. S. R. Bastard (Chairman), Mr. C. G. Lush, Mr. Walter Wethered.

Secretary.—Mr. Newman M. Ogle.

Registered Offices.—Friars House, New Broad Street, London, E.C.

This syndicate owns the following properties in the Bauchi Province:—

Rein.—An exclusive licence to prospect an area of 4½ square miles near the towns of Rein and Forum.

South Bukeru.—An exclusive licence to prospect an area of 3 square miles south of Bukeru, and sold to the company of that name.

Shen.—A mining licence to work an area of 24 acres on the left bank of the Shen stream.

The Rein property is situated on the south-eastern side of the Bauchi Tin Fields, between the pagan towns of Forum and Rein. The area encloses about six miles of a stream flowing in the northerly direction from Rein to Forum, where it junctions with a system of rivers on which the Ribon, Bisichi, Doss, and other properties are situated.

The area is three-quarters of a mile wide by six miles long, an extent of 4½ square miles, practically the whole of which is tin-bearing alluvial. The alluvial is composed of a sandy material of an extremely free nature, and the bottom is the usual coarse grey granite. The latter outcrops in very few places, and carries from about a yard to four yards of alluvial ground. Although the bottom could be reached in only a few places in the stream bed, good prospects of black tin were obtained in nearly all samples panned, and from the alluvial flats, as exposed by the banks of the stream, the results ran from about 3 to 5 lbs. of tin per cubic yard. The panning concentrates contained 10 to 15 per cent. of titaniferous iron sand (which was allowed for), but this mineral presents no difficulties, and can be easily eliminated by the ordinary dressing operations.

The width of the property (three-quarters of a mile) does not include the whole of the large alluvial flats that occur on either side of the river, but having secured the river and so much of the adjacent ground, these flats are protected, and, if necessary, may be taken up when the land for mining purposes is selected.

Of the area staked, certainly more than two-thirds carries alluvial ground of the thickness given above. Except in the bed of the stream, rich patches are not expected, but a fairly uniform value throughout.

Water.—There is a continuous flow of water for sluicing purposes all the year round.

Grades.—Cannot be determined without survey, but at the lower (Forum) end of the property there is sufficient fall to allow the tailings to be inexpensively dealt with.

Costs.—Will compare favourably with other mines in the district, *i.e.* with ground of moderate value the costs would amount to between £10 and £15 per ton of black tin, and present transport charges £27 10s. per ton inclusive.

Final tests of the flats are capable of being cheaply and quickly carried out by means of trial pits; boring is unnecessary. The probability is that the workable ground will prove to be of too large an area to be included in one mining lease, and that it will be necessary to split the present area into two or more properties.

Shen Property.—This property is situated on the left bank of the Shen stream, on which it has been pegged out for some distance with an average width of about two chains. The Shen property adjoins the concession acquired by the Bisichi Tin Company (Nigeria), Ltd.

South Bukeru.—This property, comprising an area of three square miles, is situated about four miles south of Bukeru. It is situated on the top of the Bukeru watershed, a basin heavily watered with small streams running through the whole area, which is stated to be alluvial, and all the ground is tin-bearing from the top to the bottom of the pits, which have been sunk to a depth of about fifteen feet. Pump or boring plant will be necessary to thoroughly test the property. This property has been sold to the South Bukeru (Nigeria) Tin Co., Ltd.

NIGERIA TIN CORPORATION, Ltd.

Capital.—£100,000 in 100,000 shares of £1 each; 34,782 issued; a further 25,000 are under option at 25s. per share until December 31, 1910.

Directors.—Oliver Wethered (Chairman), H. C. Godfray, R. J. Hoffmann, H. J. Moir, C. V. Thomas.

Secretary.—George Kerr, A.C.I.S.

Offices.—Capel House, 54 New Broad Street, E.C.

This company owns four areas aggregating 14 square miles in Nigeria, and in addition to these has large holdings of shares in the leading companies operating in this field, including:

Champion Gold Reefs of West Africa, Ltd.

Naraguta (Nigeria) Tin Mines, Ltd.

Juga Tin and Power Company, Ltd.

Anglo-Continental Mines, Ltd.

Northern Nigeria (Bauchi) Tin Mines, Ltd.

Another of the company's assets to which considerable importance is attached is the interest in the Juga (Nigeria) Tin and Power Company, whose property comprises what is known as the Juga area, situated on a plateau 3,280 feet above sea-level, amounting to 1,600 acres, and the Sub-Juga area which, as its name implies, is situated upon the lower plateau immediately below Juga, amounting to 6,720 acres. A further property, known as the South Juga, has also been acquired. From August 15 to September 10 the quantity of crude tin produced by the Juga Company was 12,339 lbs., but Mr. C. G. Lush, the consulting engineer, states that, as in the case of the Naraguta property, the bed of the river, in which the richest deposits of tin are contained, is exposed for calabashing in the dry season, which is now beginning, so that a much larger output of tin may be confidently expected in the near future. New plant is now being supplied capable of dressing twelve tons of tin oxide per day.

The Anglo-Continental Mines Company is largely interested in what are undoubtedly the best gold mines in the Tarkwa and Prestea, districts of West Africa, but it has also a substantial slice of the Nigerian "cake." It has already had one profitable "deal" in the successful flotation of the Northern Nigeria (Bauchi) Tin Mines, Ltd.—a company holding prospecting licences over a compact block of 50 square miles in the Bauchi Province, and mining licences over three blocks of about 12½ acres each. Portions of the property have been worked sufficiently by the Niger Company to prove their exceptional value as tin-bearing areas. Mr. C. G. Lush, reporting in February last, stated: "From surface pannings I should estimate the over-burden, or rather stanniferous gravelly deposit overlying the wash, to go 2 lbs. per cubic yard.... Provided sufficient power is obtained, there is room here for at least four big plants capable of treating 10,000 cubic yards of gravel each per week. 40,000 yards at 2 lbs. equals 80,000 lbs. of tin oxide, equal to 35 tons per week, which, at £80, means £2,800; less cost of treatment at 6d. per yard £1,000, carriage on 35 tons of tin (at £15) £525, Government royalty at 10 per cent. £127, leaving a net weekly profit of £1,148." The Anglo-Continental Mines Company has a large interest in this company, and is looking for big dividends therefrom in the not very distant future. But this is not by any means the full extent of its interest in Northern Nigeria, for it has acquired an adjoining area of 50 square miles, which are stated to afford equally satisfactory prospects.

Apart from the indirect interest the Nigerian Tin Corporation has in the Northern Nigeria (Bauchi) Tin Mines, through the Anglo-Continental Mines Company already referred to, it has a large holding on its own account.

The original intention, when the Nigerian Tin Corporation was formed, was that it should confine itself entirely to taking participation in deals and promotions, but feeling persuaded that this is the most important virgin tin field the world has yet seen, the directors decided to extend the scope of the corporation's operations, and, as already stated, four areas have been acquired of eight, three, two, and one square miles respectively.

Mr. H. O. Crighton, late manager of the Pusing Lama Mine, in the Straits Settlements, has been appointed the company's manager in Northern Nigeria in January last, and has already taken up three areas on behalf of this company.

NORTHERN NIGERIA (BAUCHI) TIN MINES, Ltd.

Capital.—£200,000 in £1 shares, of which 169,000 are issued and fully paid, including 100,000 given in part payment of the property.

Directors.—Sir Robert A. Hampson, J.P. (Chairman), Mr. Hugh C. Godfray, Mr. George T. Harris, Mr. Oliver Wethered, and Mr. Hetherington White.

Secretary.—Mr. E. Price.

This company has exclusive prospecting rights over an area of 50 square miles in the Naraguta district of Northern Nigeria, together with mining licences over a further area of 12½ acres situated at the head-waters of a small river.

The manager of this company in Nigeria is Mr. Means, who has done a considerable amount of prospecting on the property. This large property of 50 square miles was originally secured by the Anglo-Continental Company. It is believed there are several large areas of alluvial tin on the property, which has not yet been properly prospected.

With regard to the smaller concession of 12½ acres, Mr. Lush confirmed the statement that the alluvial tin at this point was exceptionally rich, averaging as much as 12 lbs. per cubic yard.

In his report on this property dated February 21, 1910, Mr. Lush said:

"From surface pannings I should estimate the overburden, or rather stanniferous gravelly deposit overlying the wash, to go 2 lbs. per cubic yard. It would be interesting to see the values and thickness of the bottom wash. Provided sufficient power is obtained, there is room here for at least four big plants capable of treating 10,000 cubic yards of gravel each per week: 40,000 yards at 2 lbs. equals 80,000 lbs. of tin oxide, equal to 35 tons per week.

"I look for a fair depth of payable ground, everything points to its being so, but only boring can decide this.

"Life of property would largely depend on the depth of the

deposit and the number of plants erected, but presuming the deposit is 15 feet deep, and you instal four plants capable of putting through 10,000 yards weekly each, it would take fully eight years to work out this 500 acres of the property.

"I understand that the total area of land taken over by you from the Niger Bauchi Syndicate is 50 square miles, or 32,000 acres. In this report I am only dealing with the southern and south-western part of your holding, some 20 square miles, as I did not visit the northern portion. I was, however, credibly informed by one of the Government mining officials that on the northern block of 30 square miles there are also stanniferous deposits, and in addition a very promising tin lode, a continuation of the one that has been opened up by the Niger Company on your eastern boundary. The actual value and life of only the area I have reported upon would, in my opinion, quite justify your proceeding with vigorous development work at once. The probable values of the remaining 30 square miles may possibly turn out equal to the southern; there is no reason why they should not, as the whole of the property is within a rich alluvial and lode tin district that has hardly as yet been scratched."

On June 15 the company's representative in Nigeria cabled: "Active sluicing operations will be commenced as soon as sufficient water is available. Meantime 6 tons of tin have been produced by means of calabashes."

A complete sluicing plant has been shipped, and pending its arrival washing by means of calabashes is being continued.

At the first statutory meeting, Mr. Lush said, since delivering his report:

"I see by a cablegram from Mr. Means that he has found

good tin on other areas. There are about 4 square miles of about 2,600 acres that have been proved to carry tin since I left there."

REPORT ON THE N'GELL RIVER TIN DEPOSITS, NORTHERN NIGERIA

By Mr. H. W. Laws

The N'Gell River, which is one of the sources of the Kaduna, rises in the pagan town of N'Gell on the highest watershed of the country.

Black oxide of tin is found in large quantities in the bed of this river where it is not deeply covered with gravel, and in the various streams flowing into it, especially those coming in from the south. The ore undoubtedly has a very local origin, it is derived largely from the denudation of the small tin-bearing quartz veins in pegmatite granite on the sources of the tributaries known as Nos. 1 and 2 streams, and lode matter containing massive crystals of tin is also breaking down in the neighbourhood of Nos. 4 and 5 streams. All these it will be noted are on the south side of the river.

For the purpose of discussing these tin deposits as a mining proposition, the river may be conveniently divided into three portions:

A. The headwaters of the N'Gell River (sections 49 and 50 on plan) with Nos. 1, 2, and 3 streams.

B. The portion of the N'Gell River flowing through the Niger Company's area for a distance of 2½ miles with the tributaries known as Nos. 4, 5, and 6 streams, and

C. The portion of the N'Gell River flowing for a distance of six miles through section 46 and 36 to 40 on the plan.

A

This portion is actually on the apex of the watershed. The streams which fall rapidly to the valley below on the west are crossed by numerous bars of granite and quartz reefs, which act as natural riffles, and have served to concentrate the ore in high values, but relatively small quantities of alluvial in the beds and banks of the streams. Good alluvial also occurs in patches amongst the granite hills away from the waterways.

The streams get a fairly regular supply of water from springs and the drainage of the many veins, but they are also subject to scouring floods caused by heavy but entirely local rains. The floods are breaking down the alluvial with great rapidity, and large quantities of ore must be washed down to the valley below every year.

During three months of somewhat irregular work last year we recovered 30 tons of black tin from Nos. 1 and 2 streams. Part of this was won by sluicing the alluvial banks, of which 2,736 cubic yards, worth 10 to 11 lbs. of black tin per yard, were worked. Operations were commenced from the boundary, the ground was worked fairly, and although superficially it only represents some 300 square yards, it gives a fair idea of the value of the bank deposits. The values, of course, would not apply to the alluvial apart from the streams, nor to that on No. 3 stream, where there is far less grade and more alluvial, but, taken as a whole, the proposition is decidedly the richest yet found in Nigeria. Until further prospecting has been done and a detailed survey carried out, it is impossible to give any accurate estimate of the payable alluvial available on this portion; as a hand-work proposition it is not of great extent (as will be gathered from my report to the Niger Company last December, a copy of which I attach), but as an area systematically worked with the aid of machinery, it is undoubtedly a property which should produce a large tonnage of tin over a period of many years.

The above-mentioned report also clearly sets forth the difficulties in the way of systematic mining, if it is to be regarded as a separate concern. I have carefully considered the methods suggested by Mr. Lush in his report. The first we have already tried. The second is impracticable, because we have no higher level at which we could conserve water for hydraulicing the whole of the alluvial deposits, and the third and fourth can only be considered in conjunction with one or both of the other portions of the N'Gell River.

A modification of the second suggestion might prove satisfactory as a temporary measure. It would be possible to conserve in a reservoir constructed near the head of one of the streams sufficient water to sluice by gravity—I do not think there would be pressure for hydraulicing—the alluvial in and near the main river and part of that about the three streams. The ground higher up the streams could not be worked by this means.

B

This portion of the river flows through the Niger Company's area, as shown on the plan attached. The river, after leaving the town of N'Gell, falls into a fine open valley within which is an apparently deep basin filled in with loose gravels heavily charged with water.

Four important streams numbered 3, 4, 5, and 6, enter the

river from the south, three of them having falls in the position marked on the plan.

In addition to the alluvial being washed down the main stream, this basin must also be enriched by the tin-bearing wash in the tributaries, which also show good prospects.

The basin covers an area of roughly 300 acres, not including the bank deposits on the streams or the higher level flats. As would be expected from the nature of the ground, the top gravels do not carry payable values, but it seems to me almost impossible for the bottom to be other than rich when it is remembered that tin will not travel far without easy outlet and good grades, and that for a long period tin-bearing dirt has been emptying itself into this basin from so many channels. We have been unable to reach bottom in ordinary trial pits owing to heavy water and the running nature of the alluvial, and it will now have to be tested by boring.

Even if it proves only a low-grade show, it is obviously a big mine, and one that must be worked by dredging or pumping methods. Possibly the three falls above mentioned would give sufficient power, in which case the problem of working the "A" deposits would be solved at the same time. Otherwise it would be necessary to acquire the Kwall Falls, and generate electric power there.

C

I am not so familiar with this portion of the river, but, generally speaking, it is of a similar character to "B," and the same remarks apply, but with this important exception, that it is down stream and therefore farther away from the source of the tin. I am not in a position to say whether it is fed by other tin-bearing streams or rocks further to the west.

As your Chairman very reasonably suggested, there may be an obstruction in the shape of rising bedrock or bars about Section 46, in which case this portion may prove of little value. This can only be disclosed by continuing the boring operations, and I would here emphasise Mr. Lush's opinion that the greatest care should be exercised in taking samples from holes in these loose gravels where boring has a tendency to concentrate the heavier mineral at the bottom.

RECOMMENDATIONS

As some difficulty is anticipated in holding the areas as they now stand after this year, I suggest that they be dealt with as follows:—

> (A) The streams and alluvial deposits on this portion are spread over some six square miles of country, so that my previous suggestion that the whole should be taken up in one rectangular mining area is not feasible. A mining area should be acquired over Sections 49 and 50 as under:—
>
> Commencing at the N'Gell Beacon, thence 2 miles due west, thence 1 mile due north, thence 2 miles due east, and thence 1 mile due south to the starting point, enclosing an area of 2 square miles.
>
> Mining licences over Nos. 1, 2, and 3 streams should be renewed.

The above four mining areas will not include all the alluvial mentioned in this report as existing on this portion (A), but if the three streams are held, the alluvial lying between them will be safe from others, who would have no water for working it. This is only intended to meet the case temporarily, and until further surveys have been made and the Mining Laws revised.

(B) Negotiations should be entered into with the Niger Company to take over this part of the river, or with a view to an amalgamation of interests.

A mining licence should then be obtained to commence at a beacon 10,343 feet due west of the N'Gell beacon, thence 2½ miles due west, thence 1 mile due south, thence 2½ miles due east, thence 1 mile due north to the starting point, enclosing an area of 2½ square miles.

(C) I recommend that an exclusive prospecting licence be applied for, identical with Sections 36 to 40, enclosing an area of five square miles. If a prospecting licence is not allowed in any form, the expense of holding this piece of land under mining licences must be borne until prospecting is completed.

There remains only the river flowing through Sections 46 and 35. A rectangular prospecting area (or, if refused, a mining area) ½ mile wide, east and west, by about 1¼ miles long, north and south, will be sufficient to hold this while its examination is going on.

With regard to staff and the work for the immediate future, a good surveyor and assistant must be sent out whose chief duty, apart from the demarcation of boundaries, would be the determination of grades in the rivers, measurement of water, survey of falls, and the preparation of sections showing the alluvial beds as disclosed by the pits and bores. An experienced man to carry out the boring operations should also be provided, and the whole work placed in charge of a capable hydraulic mining engineer.

CONCLUSION

It is above all things desirable to aim at working the whole of the deposits about this river as one large power proposition, deriving the power either from falls on the property or from Kwall. Should it be found impossible to do this (from failure to secure the land and falls required), then it will have to be proved whether the deposits on the six square miles of "A" portion justify the expense of harnessing falls and conveying power to the heads of the streams. If not, as much of the alluvial as possible must be worked out by the same system of sluicing as was employed last year, but on an increased scale, and with a more elaborate method of dealing with the water supply.

I am of opinion that it will take a year with a competent staff to prove the six miles of land referred to in "A" portion.

(Signed) H. W. LAWS, M.I.M.M.

3rd September, 1910.

N'GELL STREAM AREAS

28th December, 1909.

The Secretary,
NIGER COMPANY, LIMITED,
LONDON, W.C.

DEAR SIR,—I beg to hand you herewith Summary of tin returns for the months of November and December.

Tin Recovery.—Work ceased on the 14th instant owing to Mr. Carpenter's time being completed, and his desire to return to England; otherwise sluicing on No. 1 stream could have continued to the end of the year. Sluicing on No. 2 stream was stopped early in November owing to want of water.

The black tin recovered for November amounted to 12 tons and 2 lbs., and from December 1st to 14th, 4 tons 14 cwts. 3 qrs. 12 lbs., making a total of 30 tons 0 cwts. 1 qr. 3 lbs. for the three months that mining operations have been carried on, as shown on the summary.

The ground sluiced at No. 1 stream measures approximately 2,736 cubic yards, worth 10 to 11 lbs. of black tin per cubic yard.

In arriving at these figures, the tin taken from the actual river bed, where it was impossible to measure the ground sluiced, is excluded, and this value will be found to be a fair average for the alluvial bank deposits on the N'Gell areas.

I estimate there is sufficient of this to last for six years on the two areas we have taken up, but this does not include some fairly extensive deposits between the three N'Gell streams and outside our small mining leases, which we have recently found to exist. We have not attempted to develop these higher deposits, but wherever tried they carry good values, and if by careful selection we added them to the existing areas, the proposition would become an important one as far as quantity is concerned. The difficulty lies in economical working. The present method, although profitable, is unsatisfactory, at any rate from an engineering point of view; my experience of the last three months has proved that sluicing in a small way can only proceed between seasons—in the dry season only hand-work can be done, and at the height of the rains the sluices cannot be fixed low enough to receive the sluicing water. It is essentially an elevating proposition, but without power, fuel, or water, we are helpless. I therefore recommend you, should an opportunity occur, to give careful consideration to any amalgamation scheme which our neighbours on the N'Gell River might think desirable after they become familiar with their property, especially if they decide to work on a large scale.

Should no opportunity of the kind occur, I advise you to take the best out of the three streams and their alluvial banks by our present cheap sluicing methods and handwork during the next six years or so. A good engineer and an assistant would be required to supervise, but the former would only be required at certain seasons and not permanently on the property. I am preparing a list of plant required to work economically on these lines on the three streams.

Export.—The tin won was all first grade, assaying 72 per cent. to 73 per cent. 644 bags, weighing net 19 tons 9 cwts. 3 qrs. 7 lbs., were despatched in November, and 350 bags, weighing net 10 tons 10 cwts. 1 qr. 24 lbs., were despatched this month, making a total of 30 tons 0 cwts. 1 qr. 3 lbs.

General.—The plant has been properly laid up and protected from the weather for the dry season, and a watchman has been placed in charge.

I am, &c.,

(*Signed*) H. W. LAWS.

Since the preparation of the foregoing particulars a report has been received from the company's manager giving the first detailed particulars of the prospecting as follows:—

"*Prospecting.*—With regard to this important subject I expect to have a little more to say when I have a general map ready to forward to you. The shaft in Section 26 which you asked about in your letter of 26th July was not got down to bedrock on account of water, and there were no results to report. In prospecting the streams of the central and northern part of the 40-mile area, we found tin in many places in various quantities, and irregularly distributed. Apparently the best stream is that one which runs through Section 28; while prospecting there we calabashed out five tons very easily from the bed of the stream, which tin we have in stock and shall report it to the Government as soon as the mining lease is applied for. The prospecting by numerous pits shows that the ground is too irregular in values outside the bed of the stream to make satisfactory estimates until some sluicing is done, which will be a relatively easy matter when we have the mining lease. There is another stream about three miles further north which I think will warrant taking up, but perhaps not quite so good as that in Section 28.

"In prospecting other streams of the northern part of the 40-mile area we generally found from a trace of tin to say a pound or so per yard with limited yardage, and none of them offer much encouragement to the company for mining purposes.

"A part of the N'Gell River, in Sections 49 to 50, I think is suitable for taking up as a mining lease. The tin, however, appears to be mostly confined to the river bed, and therefore it is more suitable for calabashing than for sluicing purposes. Also the parts of streams Nos. 1 and 2, which are in the prospecting area, should be included in the areas applied for."

The manager further states, in regard to the drilling operations which are being carried out on the more remote and westerly portion of the property, that the results hitherto obtained have not been very encouraging, but that it is too early to arrive at a definite conclusion in regard to final results.

Cable advice has been received of the recovery of ten tons of tin during the month of October. The manager adds that the water is falling rapidly; this should permit of calabashing on an extended scale. The value of the tin already won by intermittent working should realise nearly £4,000, a sum in excess of the outlay in respect of the surveying and prospecting on which the small staff has been principally occupied.

TIN AREAS OF NIGERIA, Ltd.

Capital.—£60,000 in 240,000 shares of 5s. each.

Directors.—Assheton Leaver (Chairman), Cyril D'Arcy Leaver, James Ramsay Parsons, Franklin Stokes Saunders, Lewis Norman Way.

Secretary.—Henry Thomas Miller.

Offices.—St. Bartholomew House, 58 West Smithfield, E.C.

This company owns two alluvial tin properties of about one square mile each, and when the company was formed they had a further option for an area of about 1,920 acres, which option has since been exercised, and the property referred to in it floated as a subsidiary company called the Jos Tin Area (Nigeria) Limited.

For the purpose of identification the two properties owned by the company were described as Jos No. 2 and the Fusa property.

Mr. Malcolm has been appointed manager of the properties, and on behalf of the company has applied for and secured permission to take up a further area on the Fefan River.

Mr. S. W. Carpenter, who was in the employ of the Niger Company for five years, has been appointed engineer. Mr. A. Higgins, who has also joined this company, was formerly in the Public Works Department of Nigeria, and has been in the country for the past ten years. He will make his headquarters at Lokoja, in which place the company has contracted to acquire a site and buildings to be used for trading, with a steam launch and two barges on the river. In connection with this trading and transport work, the company have acquired properties in Nigeria belonging to the firm of Messrs. Siegler & Co., and their place in Lokoja occupies the best river site there.

This company promoted its first subsidiary company in May 1910, and was called the Jos Tin Area (Nigeria) Limited. The property was a producing one.

ANGLO-CONTINENTAL MINES CO., Ltd.

Capital.—£200,000 in 400,000 10s. shares, of which 300,000 are issued and fully paid.

Directors.—Messrs. W. F. Turner (Chairman), Edmund Davis, J. Schaar, and H. White.

Secretary.—Mr. A. W. Berry.

Offices.—22 Austin Friars, E.C.

This company, in addition to having interests in various West African and South African concerns, is interested in the Nigerian Tin Fields, and in addition to holding share interest in various companies, they have a prospecting right over an area of 50 square miles in the Bauchi district to the west of the Naraguta area, and to the north and adjoining the area of the Northern Nigeria (Bauchi) Tin Mines, Limited.

JOS TIN AREA (NIGERIA), Ltd.

Capital.—£110,000 in 440,000 shares of 5s. each.

Directors.—Assheton Leaver (Chairman), C. D'Arcy Leaver, H. T. Miller, J. R. Parsons, F. S. Saunders, A. T. Schmidt, L. N. Way.

Offices.—58 West Smithfield, E.C.

The company acquired from the Tin Areas of Nigeria Limited, an area of 1,920 acres which were originally held by the Niger Company. Mr. Charles Scott has been engaged as mine manager, and is now on the property, from which about 20 tons of black tin were won during May, June, and July.

At the statutory meeting held on 22nd August, the chairman said:

"I may say that I have had the pleasure on two or three occasions of meeting Mr. H. W. Laws, who was the chief mining engineer of the Niger Company in Northern Nigeria, and is now their consulting engineer here. He had for some time the direction of the work on this particular mine. In the course of friendly conversations with him, he told me that he was of opinion that our company should get back its capital, together with interest commensurate with the risk run in all mining enterprises. He also told me that he considered the mine could go on producing indefinitely anything up to 200 tons of tin per annum, without any capital expenditure, but he added that he thought that would be a very wrong policy to pursue, and that the right thing to do was to have, as we intend having, a thorough survey made of the property, and then come to a conclusion as to the best method of working it. I think that it is very satisfactory to hear this from Mr. Laws, because it points to the fact that we have really got a sound property, and one which, if properly managed, will prove to be a sound speculative investment. It is a property which must be regarded as a low-grade proposition. Although, of course, it is more fascinating to have a property which may be called a very rich one, yet a large low-grade property is really far more satisfactory from the shareholders' point of view than a property which is simply rich in patches, because with a large low-grade proposition it is a case of "cut and come again" and as often as you like. There is always something to go away with. Mr. Lush, in a report which he gave us at the time of the flotation of this mine, estimated that we could reckon upon having 500 acres containing 2 lbs. of tin per cubic yard, and if that estimate is realised—and I have no reason to anticipate that it will not be realised—and the profits are made that he foreshadowed might be made, you have a very handsome property, and one containing apparently something over half a million sterling worth of tin."

BISICHI TIN COMPANY (NIGERIA), Ltd.

Capital.—£200,000 in £1 shares.

Directors.—The Earl of Wharncliffe, Sir William Wallace, K.C.M.G., William Scott Coutts, Samuel Watkin Carlton, James Gardiner.

Secretary.—Stanley Aldous.

Offices.—51 and 52 Fenchurch Street, E.C.

This company was formed to acquire and work mining rights over a property known as the Bisichi Valley Tin Area, comprising an area of three square miles in extent, situated in the Bauchi Tin Fields. It is located about 12 miles south-east of Jos, at the head-waters of the river Gongola, on the main transport route from Keffi to Naraguta.

Mr. Laws, the general mining manager of the Niger Company, in his report, says:

"One of the most pleasing features of this property is its constant supply of water for sluicing and power purposes, and the ample head of water given by the three falls for hydraulicing."

In the Bisichi Valley there is a large alluvial deposit of light sandy material which is quite free from clay, and is extremely friable, and consequently capable of cheap and rapid concentration.

Black oxide of tin occurs abundantly in the river beds and adjacent alluvial flats, and is of very good quality, there being practically no iron or other impurity associated with it. The tin-bearing alluvial is all on the surface, and varies in depth from a few inches to some 20 feet in the vicinity of the river.

Systematic tests of the alluvial by trial pits were commenced this year, and up to the present the great proportion of the alluvial of the river Bisichi has been tested.

The tested ground averages 4 yards in depth, and contains approximately 2,120,000 cubic yards of payable alluvial wash. The latter varies in value from traces to 129 lbs. of black tin per cubic yard, the average value being 7.27 lbs. of black tin per cubic yard. The total contents of the tested portion therefore amounts to 6,800 tons, exclusive of the river bed deposits, which the Niger Company's engineers estimate to contain about 1,000 tons.

The nature of the river-bed wash does not lend itself to accurate sampling, but Mr. Laws, judging by actual returns from similar deposits on this field, considers this estimate of 1,000 tons a moderate one, and states that it may be taken that some 7,800 tons of black tin (containing over 70 per cent. of pure metal) have been developed to date. Taking the costs as estimated by Mr. Laws at £45 per ton, the above tonnage contained in the area already proved, shows an available profit of over £350,000.

Payable tin-bearing alluvial exists on other portions of the Bisichi Valley area, but as it has not yet been measured or tested, no exact estimate can be made of quantities and values. The ground already tested represents about one-tenth of the total area; but the very high values and quantities so far disclosed cannot be taken to apply to the whole area, as it is natural that the course of the main stream should carry better values and deeper ground than the remainder of the land where the alluvial would be more patchy and shallower. It will be seen, however, that the estimated working costs per ton have been placed by Mr. Laws at a figure which will permit of lower grade ground being worked than that already referred to.

Mr. Laws advises the immediate erection of an hydraulicing plant capable of dealing efficiently with wash dirt sufficient to produce 800 tons of black tin annually, an ample head of water being available for this purpose throughout the year.

He also states that it would be quite possible to commence work on the property immediately by ground sluicing; but he is strongly of opinion that this policy would be unwise, as the disturbance of the ground might tend to interfere with the economical working on a large scale such as is proposed.

Provided no unforeseen difficulties arise, Mr. Laws is of opinion that the whole of the plant would be in operation within nine months.

If Mr. Laws' advice is taken, he estimates that working cost would amount to about £10 per ton on ore of the value already found, but, as stated above, to allow for working a larger quantity of lower grade ground, working costs should be placed at £15 per ton of ore. The price of the ore in the market at Liverpool may be taken at £90 per ton, which, after deducting £15 for working costs, and £30 per ton for transport and contingencies, would leave a margin of profit of £45 per ton of ore. Although it is proposed in the earlier stages of development to equip the mine with plant capable of producing 800 tons annually, any increase on this rate of working will depend on surveys determining the head of water available.

WEST AFRICAN MINES, Ltd.

Capital.—£100,200 in £1 shares, of which 100,000 are ordinary shares and 200 founders' shares; all are issued and fully paid.

Directors.—Rt. Hon. Lord Harris (Chairman), Edmund Davis, Friedrich Eckstein, H. Strakosah, R. G. Fricker (Managing Director).

Secretaries.—The Consolidated Goldfields of South Africa, Limited.

Offices.—8 Old Jewry, E.C.

This company, which is managed by the Consolidated

Goldfields of South Africa, Limited, has secured an interest in a tin business in Nigeria. The company have sent out Mr. Balfour, who has had experience in tin dredging in the Straits Settlements. The tin property which is here referred to was floated in conjunction with the Anglo-Continental Mines, Limited, and was called the Northern Nigerian (Bauchi) Tin Mines, Limited.

BENUE (NORTHERN NIGERIA) TIN MINES, Ltd.

Capital.—£10,000 in £1 shares; 8,500 are issued and fully paid, the balance are under option at par till 31st March, 1911.

Directors.—Charles E. Pearson (Chairman), C. L. W. Wallace, H. Kemble, G. F. Jones.

Secretary.—J. H. Dormer.

Offices.—21 Great Winchester Street, E.C.

The company originally held a prospecting mining licence over an area of ten square miles, situated in the Benue River district, Northern Nigeria.

Mr. Harry Kemble, accompanied by an experienced engineer, left for Nigeria early this year. The following circular was issued to the shareholders on 29th August 1910:

"I beg to inform you that Mr. Kemble, writing from Naraguta, on 21st July, reports as follows:—

"'Please inform my brother-directors I have acquired four square miles of very rich tin area, as stated in my cable of the 19th inst. It is mainly in the streams, and will be almost entirely recovered by calabash washing (*i.e.* natives washing the alluvial in calabashes).'"

In a cable from Mr. Kemble, dated 8th August, he states that he has acquired a further six square miles, also rich, and on 21st August he cabled that he has acquired "another square mile extremely rich."

With regard to the exact locality of these areas, Mr. Kemble says: "Mr. Knight will have plans, report, &c., ready for sending home as soon as possible."

The following was issued to shareholders on 15th September 1910:

"Referring to my circular of 29th August, in which I informed you that Mr. H. Kemble reported having secured in all eleven square miles of very rich tin area, in a letter just received from Mr. Kemble, dated 3rd August, he states that as a test they have washed 3,000 lbs. of tin in five days' work. With reference to seven square miles which Mr. Kemble has secured for the company, he says:

"'(1) Property on which camp is built lies nearly half-way between Bauchi Town and Naraguta. It is two miles long by half-mile wide, taking in the Ademi River in its length. There are other smaller streams on the property running into the Ademi, and also containing tin. One square mile. (2) Property on the river known locally as the Kogin Zungur, one day's march due south of Bauchi Town, and commencing quarter-mile south-west of the town of Zungur, is six miles long and one wide. Mr. Knight reports it rich in tin. Six square miles. It is impossible for Mr. Knight to make detailed plans yet, as all his time must be devoted to getting hold of further concessions.'"

GEL TIN LODE AND ALLUVIAL COMPANY, Ltd.

Capital.—£100,000 in 400,000 shares of 5s. each; present issue 240,000 shares.

Directors.—Mr. P. G. Hamilton-Carvill, J.P. (Director of the Van Ryn Gold Mining Estates, Ltd.), Mr. T. F. Dalglish (Director of the Taquah and Abosso Gold Mining Cos.), Mr. James A. Duncan (Director of New African Co., Ltd.), Mr. Leama R. Davis (Director of Millar's Karri and Jarrah Co., Ltd.), and Mr. George Ochs (Director of Abosso Gold Mining Co.).

Secretary.—Mr. H. J. Smith.

Offices.—34 Clement's Lane, E.C.

This company has secured an area of 5¼ miles next to Naraguta, the alluvial area comprising about 785 acres. Mr. H. W. Laws reporting on these 785 acres, says:

"The bed of the stream is extremely rich in tin, in fact it is one of the richest in the country."

Mr. Laws also says that fifty natives with calabashes can earn 10 tons of tin per month at a cost of less than £10 per ton, and that the extra expense for transport, &c., to England, would not come to more than £30. This would mean that fifty tributers, with the most primitive methods, could earn 100 tons per annum, since it is stated that there is plenty of water for sluicing purposes during eight months of the year. During the remaining four dry months of the year there is ample water left in the pools. In addition to the alluvial properties, the Gel Company has a half share in a lode firm on a property covering 640 acres. Upon this lode the Niger Company have already spent £10,000 in prospecting shafts with satisfactory results. The lode formation is 20 feet wide on an average, and an analysis of prospects gave 20 per cent. of tin.

AKERRI (NIGERIA) TIN COMPANY, Ltd.

Capital.—£125,000 in £1 shares, issued as fully paid in part payment of purchase money; 25,000 were offered at par, and are 2s. paid, and the remaining 35,500 are held in reserve for future issue.

Directors.—Mr. Charles Vivian Thomas (Chairman of Tronoh Mines), Mr. Arthur Oliphant Burton, Mr. Louis A. Neel.

Secretary.—Mr. C. M. Champness, C.A.

Offices.—103 Cannon Street, E.C.

This company acquired their property through Mr. W. H. Champion, who has also reported on the property. Most of the other companies which have been formed up to this date, are working in the Bauchi Province, and as the Akerri Company is proposing to work in a new district near Zungeru, the present capital of the Colony, a copy of Mr. Champion's report is given in full:

"Having been appointed by you to prospect and report on your tin properties in Northern Nigeria, to which place I proceeded in March, I have now much pleasure in submitting to you the following particulars:

"*Situation.*—Your property is situate one day's journey in a south-westerly direction from Zungeru, the present capital of the Colony, and one and a half day's journey north-east of Jebba, which is an important railway centre.

"There is one important point as regards its position, which places it far ahead of any property of any company at present working in this Colony. That is, you have as boundaries, on the north the Lagos Railway (Northern Extension), on the west the Kara River, and on the east the Kaduna River.

"It is a granite country, and although in the Naraguta district reefs have been proved to exist, large alluvial deposits, which yield cassiterite (tin oxide), are of chief importance.

"*Mining.*—For a couple of years the natives have been working in the rivers adjoining, and also on your property, treating the ore in their usual primitive way by means of 'washing' with wooden pans or calabashes.

"Under my supervision a large number of bore-holes were put down, varying in depth from 10 feet to 35 feet. I can form no idea as to the depths of the tin-bearing soil, as on the western boundary I have reached 35 feet in depth without getting to the end, on the eastern boundary about 30 feet in depth. You have over the whole of your area alluvial deposits existing on a very large scale. These deposits yield cassiterite (tin oxide) containing on an average 62 per cent. metallic tin, which proves the alluvial to be as rich or even richer than you find in any other part of the world.

"I estimate the yield at 7 lbs. per cubic yard—equal to, say, 5 s. per cubic yard, with tin oxide at £85 per ton. The cost of production would be approximately 6d. per cubic yard.

"The extent of the property is great, the natural facilities for mining are favourable, and the output of tin will be simply proportionate to the number of men employed. Assuming that a minimum of only 250 natives be employed, they should produce 500 tons of metallic tin per annum. Taking the price of tin oxide at £85 per ton, there would be a profit of some £36,000 per annum.

"The mining rights are over 3,200 acres, or five square miles, granted by the Northern Nigerian Government, and are subject to an annual rent of 5s. per acre.

"There is also a 10 per cent. royalty on the net profits derived from production, but I can assure you that there is every prospect of a reduction taking place in the near future.

"*Labour.*—This is undoubtedly one of the most important questions with which mining companies will have to deal at a very near date. This I foresaw, and am now pleased to say that arrangements have been made with the Zereki, or Chief of the Village, close by, to provide you with not less than 300 natives at any time or date, the same are required.

"*Transport.*—This is another important question.

"At the present moment the railway has not been completed, but I assure you that it will be before the end of the present year. They are now laying it at the rate of one mile per day, and are only some forty miles from your property when I left on 14th May.

"In this matter you have a very great advantage over those companies who are exploiting the Bauchi district, for, to quote the words of their expert, the cost of carriage from their tin fields to Liverpool is some £27 per ton. The cost to you will not exceed £12 per ton, so you will have on every ton arriving in Liverpool a clear profit of £15 more than they get. This is a large margin, and when worked out on the small production of 500 tons per annum (which I have previously mentioned), means a sum of £7,500 over and above what they can get on the same quantity.

"*Water.*—There is no need for me to dwell on this point, as the very large rivers you have as boundaries will be more than ample supply for all or any companies who will be operating here in the near future.

"*Climate.*—Northern Nigeria is far different to any part of West Africa. You are at an elevation of some 500 feet. The nights are quite cool, and any man who takes ordinary care of himself and lives well ought to have good health. It is, in my opinion, by far and away the healthiest part of West Africa, and I say this after sixteen years spent in different parts of it.

"In conclusion, the results obtained prove conclusively that there is immense alluvial wealth which can be cheaply won, and I believe in this property you have one which will prove an astonishing success.

"I should recommend you to at once commence operations on a large scale.

"A large working capital is unnecessary; and I consider that £25,000 will be more than ample for all requirements."

NEW AFRICAN COMPANY, Ltd.

This company, which has been dealing for some time in South African business, has recently acquired an interest in a Nigerian tin property comprising an area of 640 acres, containing a lode which is claimed to be the mother lode of the district. Arrangements are now being made to prove the lode at depth. In addition this company have also acquired an alluvial property adjoining, which runs along the bed of a stream for a distance of about 5¼ miles, and extends to a width of 200 yards on each bank. The property has as its northern neighbour the Naraguta Company, with the Jos Tin Company on the east, and the Bauchi Tin Syndicate on the west. This company appears to be working in conjunction with the Gel Tin Lode and Alluvial Company, which company is probably a subsidiary company issued by it.

THE SOUTH BUKERU (NIGERIA) TIN COMPANY, Ltd.

Capital.—£50,000, divided into 50,000 ordinary shares of £1 each, of which 20,000 are for working capital.

Directors.—Segar R. Bastard (Chairman, Champion Gold Reefs of West Africa, Ltd., and Director of Juga (Nigeria) Tin and Power Co., Ltd.), Wm. F. Jackson (1-2 Great Winchester Street, E.C., and Stock Exchange, E.C.), John Waddington, J.P. (Director, Naraguta (Nigeria) Tin Mines, Ltd.).

Consulting Engineer.—Charles G. Lush, M.E.

Secretary.—H. Tuffrey.

Offices.—Blomfield House, 85 London Wall, E.C.

This company has been formed to acquire the exclusive rights to prospect for minerals, mineral oils, and precious stones over an area of 3 square miles, situated about 4 miles south of Bukeru, in the well-known Bauchi Tin Fields of Northern Nigeria.

The property is situated on the top of the Bukeru Watershed, a basin heavily watered with small streams running through the whole area, which is stated to be alluvial, and all the ground is tin-bearing from the top to the bottom of the pits, which have been sunk to a depth of about 15 feet. Mr. Lush, the consulting engineer to the principal Nigerian tin mining companies, who thinks well of the property, has consented to act as consulting engineer for this company.

A party, consisting of four engineers with boring plant and stores, has already sailed for Nigeria to take possession of and work this property, as well as two other properties belonging to the Gongola Syndicate, Limited, and arrangements have been made for giving to this company the benefit of this organisation, on payment of a proportion of the charges incurred and to be incurred in connection therewith. There will be set aside £20,000 of the capital for working capital, of which 10,000 shares will be subscribed for immediately.

The purchase consideration is 30,000 fully-paid shares to be allotted to the Wadu Syndicate or its nominees, and the right to subscribe at par for the unissued capital of the company.

It may be mentioned that it is estimated that a profit of at least £45 per ton of ore will be obtained, taking the actual price at £90 per ton and deducting £15 for the cost of working and £30 for transport, &c., which latter item will shortly be considerably reduced.

RIBON VALLEY (NIGERIA) TIN FIELDS, Ltd.

Capital.—£200,000 in 200,000 shares of £1 each, of which 50,000 are set aside for working capital.

Directors.—Mr. Edward Hooper (Chairman), Mr. Sidney J. Messenger, Mr. Herbert Moir, Mr. James Wickett (Director of the Malay Tin Mines), and Mr. H. W. Pelham Clinton.

Secretary.—Mr. George Kerr, A.C.I.S.

Offices.—Capel House, New Broad Street, E.C.

This company has acquired a most extensive property—nine miles in extent—and holds it under an exclusive prospecting licence from the Northern Nigerian Government. So far the prospectus has only been privately issued. The licence carries with it the right to select areas for mining purposes for periods of twenty-one years, at an annual rental of 5s. per acre, and a royalty on the mineral output. The property is situated on the head-waters of the river Gongola, the river flowing through the area being locally known as the Ribon. It is about 20 miles south-east of Naraguta, and within easy reach of the main transport route. There is a constant and unlimited supply of water, and a large quantity of timber suitable for fuel. The labour is plentiful, cheap, and suitable for alluvial mining. The costs are put approximately at £20 per ton of black tin, of a minimum of 70 per cent. Mr. H. W. Laws, M.I.M.M., the chief mining engineer of the Niger Company, says: "I consider the area has excellent prospects of proving very large and profitable, and that in selecting land for mining purposes it will probably be necessary to acquire two, and perhaps three, separate leases, owing to its unusually large extent." An engineer of wide experience and an assistant has left London for the property, and Mr. Walter Wethered, who is paying his third visit to the Nigerian tin field, is to attend to the Company's interests on the spot. The intention is that the Ribon Company shall become one of the parent kind, because it is quite impossible that, unaided, it can develop so large a sett.

THE REIN RIVER (NIGERIA) TIN MINING CO., Ltd.

Capital.—£76,000, divided into 270,000 ordinary shares of 5s. each, and 170 deferred shares of 1s. each.

Directors.—S. R. Bastard, Chairman of Champion Gold Reefs of West Africa, Ltd., Lucky Chance Mines, Ltd., Tin Fields of Northern Nigeria, Ltd., South Bukeru (Nigeria) Tin Co., Ltd., Director of Juga (Nigeria) Tin and Power Co., Ltd. (Chairman).

C. G. Lush, M.E., Director of Tin Fields of Northern Nigeria, Ltd., and Goss Moor, Ltd., Consulting Engineer to South Bukeru (Nigeria) Tin Co., Ltd., and Naraguta (Nigeria) Tin Mines, Ltd.

Julius L. F. Vogel, M.I.E.E., M.I.M.M.

John Waddington, J.P., Director of Naraguta (Nigeria) Tin Mines, Ltd., Champion Gold Reefs of West Africa, Ltd., South Bukeru (Nigeria) Tin Co., Ltd., and Great Boulder Proprietary Gold Mines, Ltd.

Offices.—Friars House, New Broad Street, E.C.

This company has acquired an exclusive prospecting licence over about 1,440 acres of alluvial tin-bearing ground, situated at Forum on the Rein River, in the Province of Bauchi, which is at present the richest known tin district in Northern Nigeria. From this district alone over one thousand tons of tin have already been won. The property extends for a distance of about three miles along the river. Hand-washing by calabashes and simple sluice-boxes, using a stream of water, have been employed, and this method will be adopted by this company for the present.

ESTIMATES

By comparison with the results obtained in the district it is estimated that, when the property is opened out, an output of 50 tons a month or 600 tons a year of "Black Tin" should be obtained, and the following results may be anticipated on the basis of the report:—

Sale of 600 tons of "Black Tin" at £90 per ton (the present price being over £100 per ton)		£54,000
Cost of production (maximum estimate) at £15 per ton	£9,000	
Freight under present conditions at £29 10s. per ton	17,700	
Administration, rent, royalties, &c., about	4,300	
		31,000
Estimated nett annual profit		£23,000

By about March the new freight conditions should be in force, which would increase the estimated nett profit to about £29,000 per annum.

Life and Tonnage.—Assuming Mr. Wethered's figures that more than two-thirds of the area carries 3 to 5 lbs. per cubic yard for a depth of from 1 to 4 yards, the following is an estimate of the tonnage of tin and the life of the property:—

1,000 acres 2 yards deep at 3 lbs. per cubic yard should yield about 13,000 tons of Black Tin over about 20 years, which at £90 per ton represents a profit (taking into account reduced freight) in excess of £500,000.

Management.—An arrangement has been made with the Lucky Chance Mines Limited, for the superintendence of the company's interests, and for organising the work under a suitable manager.

The following report by Mr. Walter Wethered, one of the pioneers of the Northern Nigeria Tin Fields, was made on the original concession, which comprised an area of six miles along the river, of which this company have acquired one half.

"This property is situated on the south-eastern side of the Bauchi tin fields, between the pagan towns of Forum and Rein.

"The area encloses about six miles of a stream flowing in a northerly direction from Rein to Forum, where it junctions with the system of rivers on which the Ribon, Bisichi, Doss, and other properties are situated.

"The area is three-quarters of a mile wide by six miles long, an extent of four and a half square miles, practically the whole of which is tin-bearing alluvial. The alluvium is composed of a sandy material of an extremely free nature, and the bottom is the usual coarse grey granite. The latter outcrops in very few places, and carries from about a yard to four yards of alluvial ground. Although the bottom could be reached in only a few places in the stream bed, good prospects of black tin were obtained in nearly all samples panned, and from the alluvial flats, as exposed by the banks of the stream, the results ran from about 3 to 5 lbs. of tin per cubic yard. The panning concentrates contained 10 to 15 per cent. of titaniferous iron sand (which was allowed for), but this mineral presents no difficulty, and can be easily eliminated by the ordinary dressing operations.

"The width of the property (three-quarters of a mile) does not include the whole of the large alluvial flats that occur on either side of the river, but having secured the river and so much of the adjacent ground, these flats are protected, and, if necessary, may be taken up when the land for mining purposes is selected.

"Of the area staked, certainly more than two-thirds carries

alluvial ground of the thickness given above. Except in the bed of the stream, I would not expect rich patches, but a fairly uniform value throughout.

Water.—There is a continuous flow of water for sluicing purposes all the year round.

Grades.—Cannot be determined without survey, but at the lower (Forum) end of the property there is sufficient fall to allow the tailings to be inexpensively dealt with.

Costs.—Will compare favourably with other mines in the district, *i.e.* with ground of moderate value the costs would amount to between £10 and £15 per ton of black tin, and present transport charges £27 10s. per ton inclusive.

"Final tests of the flats are capable of being cheaply and quickly carried out by means of trial pits; boring is unnecessary. The probability is that the workable ground will prove to be of too large an area to be included in one mining lease, and that it will be necessary to split the present area into two or more properties."

NEW MINING REGULATIONS FOR NORTHERN NIGERIA

[NOTE.—The Proclamation as enacted in the Protectorate differs from this copy in the addition of a clause suspending—as regards licences to mine issued under the previous Proclamation—the operation of Section 26 and Regulation 23 (relating to royalties) until 1st January 1911, to which date the provisions of the "Minerals Proclamation, 1902," with regard to duty on profits, are kept in force.]

THE MINERALS PROCLAMATION, 1910

A Proclamation regulating the right to search for minerals and also to dig for, mine, and work minerals, and for other purposes relating thereto.

Be it enacted by the Governor of Northern Nigeria as follows:—

1. This Proclamation may be cited as "The Minerals Proclamation, 1910."

2. In this Proclamation, unless the context otherwise requires:—

"Person" includes a corporation.

"Holder" of a prospecting right or exclusive licence to prospect means the person to whom such right or licence was granted in the first instance, but in the case of an exclusive licence to prospect includes a person in whom such licence or a part of the rights thereunder has become vested by transfer, assignment, or otherwise.

"Lessee" of a mining lease includes all persons having any right or interest in or under a mining lease, whether by transfer, assignment, or otherwise.

"Treasurer" includes any officer appointed by the Governor to perform any act or duty or to exercise any authority which by this Proclamation may be done by, or is imposed upon, the Treasurer.

"Government Inspector of Mines" includes any officer appointed by the Governor to perform any act or duty or to exercise any act or authority which by this Proclamation may be done by, or is imposed upon, or may be exercised by, the Government Inspector of Mines.

Court.

"Court" means the Supreme Court or any Provincial Court.

"Minerals" means and includes the following as classed hereunder (*a*), (*b*), (*c*), and (*d*):—

(*a*) Metalliferous minerals, including antimony, arsenic, bismuth, copper, cobalt, chromium, cadmium, gold, iron, iridium, lead, manganese, mercury, molybdenum, nickel, platinum, silver, tin, tungsten, uranium, zinc, and all others of a similar nature to any of them, and all ores or combinations of any of them with each other or with any other substance, excepting only those that occur in the form of precious stones.

(*b*) Carbonaceous minerals, including anthracite, asphalt, brown coal, bitumen and its compounds, coal, graphite, lignite, and all substances of a like nature to any of them, or combinations of any of them with each other or with any other substance.

(*c*) Earthy minerals, including asbestos, barytes, clays, gypsum, infusorial earth, sandstone, marble, mica, phosphates, potash, rock salt, soda, sulphur, steatite, slate, talc, and all other substances of a like nature to any of them.

(*d*) Precious stones, including amber, amethyst, beryl, cat's eye, chrysolite, diamond, emerald, garnet, opal, ruby, sapphire, turquoise, and all substances of a similar nature to any of them.

3. Nothing in this Proclamation shall prevent any person from quarrying stone for building purposes, or any native of the Protectorate from mining for iron, salt, soda, or potash, except in any area over which a mining lease has been granted.

4.—(1) It shall not be lawful for any person to prospect for minerals without having first obtained a prospecting right or an exclusive licence to prospect in the prescribed form.

(2) An exclusive licence to prospect shall not be granted to any applicant who has not, either by himself or his duly authorised agents, examined the area over which an exclusive licence to prospect is applied for.

(3) It shall be in the discretion of the Governor for good cause to refuse an application for a prospecting right or an exclusive licence to prospect.

5. A prospecting right shall entitle the holder to prospect for any minerals in those parts of the Protectorate which are not included in any exclusive licence to prospect, and which the Governor has not by Government Notice in the Gazette declared to be closed to prospectors.

In the case of a company or corporation employing

prospecting engineers or prospectors, each prospecting engineer or prospector shall be required to take out an individual prospecting right.

6. An exclusive licence to prospect shall entitle the holder thereof, and his duly authorised agents, to the sole right of prospecting for minerals within an area not less than one square mile and not more than sixteen square miles in extent, and for a period of one year from the date thereof, subject to renewal in accordance with the prescribed regulations for further terms of one year each, but so as not to exceed a period of three years in the whole.

7. A prospecting right and an exclusive licence to prospect shall, subject to the terms thereof and to the prescribed regulations, entitle the holder thereof to enter upon any land and prospect for minerals, and any person interfering with or obstructing such holder in the exercise of any rights hereby conferred upon him shall be guilty of an offence and shall be liable to a penalty not exceeding £25 or to imprisonment for a term not exceeding three months.

8. All disputes between holders of exclusive licences to prospect in respect of the exercise of the rights granted by such licences shall be submitted through the Government Inspector of Mines to the Governor for his decision, which shall be final and conclusive between the parties: Provided always that the Governor may in his discretion refer any particular matter in dispute to a court for its decision.

9. Any person prospecting without a prospecting right or licence to prospect shall be guilty of an offence and shall on conviction before a court be liable to a penalty not exceeding £50 or to imprisonment for a term not exceeding six months.

10. A prospecting right shall not be transferable, but an exclusive licence to prospect or any portion of the rights granted under such licence may be transferred with the consent in writing of the Governor, signified by endorsement thereon.

11. In case of any breach by the holder of a prospecting right or exclusive licence to prospect or by any attorney, agent, or employee of such holder, of any of the provisions of this Proclamation or of any rule or regulation made thereunder, the Governor may summarily revoke the said right or licence and thereupon all privileges and rights conferred thereby or enjoyed thereunder shall as from the date of such revocation cease: Provided always that the fact of such revocation shall not in any way affect the liability of such holder, attorney, agent, or employee, in respect of the breach of any provision of this Proclamation or of any such rule or regulation committed by him before such revocation.

12. An exclusive licence to prospect or any portion of the rights granted under such licence may be surrendered at any time after three months' notice in writing has been given of the intention to surrender: Provided that such surrender shall not affect any liability incurred by the holder before such surrender shall have taken effect.

13.—(1) It shall not be lawful for the Governor to grant a mining lease to any person other than the holder of a prospecting right or an exclusive licence to prospect, nor to any person who cannot show to his satisfaction that he has, either himself or by his duly authorised agent, carried out *bonâ fide* prospecting operations on the area applied for.

(2) The holder of an exclusive licence to prospect who has fulfilled all the conditions attached thereto shall be entitled to

the grant of a mining lease in respect of any portion of the area covered by such licence subject to the conditions relating to the grant of such leases.

14. The Governor may require an applicant for a mining lease to show to his satisfaction that he possesses or commands sufficient working capital to ensure the proper development and working of the mine; and may require any reports on the matter made by competent engineers to be submitted for his information. In the event of such applicant failing to satisfy the Governor as aforesaid, the Governor may refuse the application, but the applicant may renew his application at any time.

15. Any applicant for a mining lease wilfully or recklessly giving false information as to any of the matters in respect of which information is or may be required to be given under this Proclamation shall be guilty of an offence, and shall be liable on conviction to a fine not exceeding £50 or to imprisonment for a term not exceeding six months.

16.—(1) A mining lease may be granted for any term not exceeding 21 years.

(2) If at the expiration of the term originally granted the lessee or his assigns shall be carrying on work in a normal and business-like manner under the lease, and the lease shall not at that time be liable to be declared void under any of the provisions of this Proclamation, and the lessee or his assigns shall have given to the Government six months' notice in that behalf, then the lessee or his assigns shall be entitled to obtain a renewal of the lease for a further term not exceeding 21 years, upon the conditions which are then generally applicable to new mining leases.

17. Mining leases shall be of the following kinds, viz.:—

(1) Lode mining leases, the unit of area being one claim of 80,000 square feet, rectangular, and of such dimensions that the width shall not be less than one-half the length. No greater area than 30 claims shall be included in one lease. The rent payable under such lease shall be at the rate of £4 per claim per annum.

(2) Alluvial mining leases, which shall not exceed 800 acres in area and shall have a minimum width throughout of 400 yards. The rent payable under such lease shall be at the rate of five shillings per acre per annum.

(3) Stream mining leases, which shall not be granted in cases where an alluvial mining lease is applicable, shall be confined to the bed of a stream and shall not exceed one mile in length. The rent payable under such lease shall be at the rate of twenty shillings per annum for each 100 yards or part thereof.

(4) Iron mining leases.

(5) Carbonaceous minerals leases.

(6) Earthy minerals and precious stones leases.

(7) Dredging leases.

> Leases of the kind (4), (5), (6), and (7) shall be granted subject to regulations to be made by the Governor under section 34 of this Proclamation.

(8) Water power leases, which shall be the subject of special agreements with the Governor; and such agreements shall make provision *inter alia*:

> (*a*) As to the rate to be charged to consumers for the supply of power, such rate to be specified in each

agreement, and not increased without the consent in writing of the Governor;

(*b*) As to the compensation to be paid by the beneficiaries thereunder in respect of interference with pre-existing individual rights of any kind whatever;

(*c*) To ensure, under penalty of revocation, the adequate development of the available power; and

(*d*) To ensure the supply of power on equitable terms to all consumers.

Provided that (1) no such agreement shall be concluded until at least three months after reasonable advertisement of the application for the lease; and (2) the Governor shall at all times have the power to determine any such agreement, subject to reasonable notice and to the payment of adequate compensation in respect of expenditure incurred.

18. The Governor may in any case where he shall deem it necessary, before granting a mining lease, require that the boundaries of the land affected shall be surveyed by a surveyor approved by the Governor, and the cost of such survey shall be paid by the person applying for the lease.

19. In the event of any areas the subject of mining leases or exclusive licences to prospect being found to overlap, the ground in dispute shall be considered as within the area first granted, and no claim, whether for compensation or otherwise, shall be allowed in respect thereof to the lessee or licensee of the area subsequently granted.

20. Every mining lease and every instrument by or under which the rights or any portion thereof granted by such lease shall

be transferred or assigned shall be registered as an instrument affecting land under the provisions of the law for the time being in force with regard to the registration of such instruments.

21. Any person digging for, mining, or working any mineral without a mining lease shall be guilty of an offence, and shall be liable upon conviction thereof to a penalty not exceeding £500 or to imprisonment for a term not exceeding twelve months.

22. The lessee of a mining lease shall be entitled to the use of all water within the area of his lease, but he shall not, without the consent in writing of the Government Inspector of Mines, treat any river or other flowing water or stream in such a manner as to prevent its return to its natural channel before it leaves the said area.

Provided that nothing herein contained shall be construed to affect or prejudice the existing rights of any person to the reasonable use of the water flowing in a natural bed or channel through, or along the margin of, land occupied by him, or naturally deposited within such land.

23. Any person diverting any river, flowing water, or stream without consent as aforesaid, or diverting water in such a manner as to render it unavailable for use by another person legally entitled to the use thereof, shall be guilty of an offence, and shall be liable to a penalty not exceeding £25, or to imprisonment for a term not exceeding three months.

24.—(1) A mining lease shall not of itself confer any rights in or over the surface of the area included in the lease, but if the lessee shall apply to the Governor for a right of occupancy over the whole or any portion of the area included in his lease, and shall show to the satisfaction of the Governor that the exclusive use and enjoyment of the said area or portion thereof is necessary to the full and effective exercise of the rights conferred by the lease, the Governor shall grant a right of occupancy over such area or portion thereof, subject to the provisions of the law for the time being in force with regard to such rights, and to such reservations as he shall think fit to make in respect of any railway, tramway, public road, building, burial-ground, or land appropriated to any public purpose, or land in the legal occupation of any other person.

(2) A right of occupancy granted as aforesaid shall run concurrently with the mining lease, and shall be renewable on application with each renewal of the mining lease, and no rent shall be payable thereunder over and above the rent payable under the mining lease; but compensation shall be payable in respect of any disturbance of native rights.

(3) In the event of any application being received from a third party for any rights in or over the surface of an area included in a mining lease, the Governor shall give notice thereof to the lessee, and if the latter shall within six months of the date of such notice show to the satisfaction of the Governor that the application cannot be granted without loss or damage to him in respect of the rights conferred by the said mining lease, the Governor shall assess reasonable compensation to be paid by the applicant to the lessee as a condition precedent to the grant of the application. If, however, the lessee shall fail to satisfy the Governor as aforesaid, the Governor may thereupon grant the application and no action shall lie in respect of any loss or damage that may ensue in respect thereof.

25. Compensation shall be made to the legal occupier by the holder of a prospecting right or exclusive licence to prospect, and by the lessee of a mining lease other than the holder of a

right of occupancy, for all damage done by himself, his agents, or employees, to the surface of any land upon, or under which prospecting or mining operations are being carried on, or to any house or building upon any such land, and the amount of such compensation shall be decided by the Resident of the province in which such land is situated: Provided that if either party is dissatisfied with the decision of such Resident he may within fourteen days appeal to the Governor, who may either decide the matter, in which case such decision shall be final, or refer it to a court for decision.

26. There shall be paid by all holders of mining leases a royalty to the Government on all ores, minerals, and metals won, which royalty shall be at such rate as may be laid down in the regulations made under section 34, and may be collected in the form of an export duty or in such manner and subject to such conditions as may be laid down in such regulations.

27. If the holder of any right acquired under this Proclamation shall consider himself injuriously affected by the mining or prospecting operations of another, he shall report the matter in writing to the Government Inspector of Mines. The Government Inspector of Mines shall forward a copy of the report to all persons concerned, and after due consideration shall give his decision thereon.

Any person may appeal from the decision of the Government Inspector of Mines to the Governor, after first notifying the Government Inspector of Mines of his intention to do so, and stating the grounds of his dissatisfaction. The Government Inspector of Mines shall at once report the matter to the Governor, who may either decide the matter himself, in which case his decision shall be final, or refer it to a court, which, upon such reference, shall decide the matter in dispute as though it came before it in the ordinary course of law.

28. No person entitled or claiming to be entitled to any rights under a prospecting right or an exclusive licence to prospect or under a mining lease shall, in the exercise of any such rights, without the consent in writing of the Governor, disturb or interfere with any railway, tramway, public road or building, burial ground or land appropriated by law to any public purpose, and any person guilty of any such disturbance or interference shall be liable on conviction before a court to a penalty not exceeding £100, and in addition may be ordered by the court to pay the costs of making good any damage caused by him.

29. If there shall be a breach on the part of the lessee of a mining lease of any condition or provision of this Proclamation or of any regulation made thereunder, or of any of the terms of his lease, and if the lessee shall not make good such breach within three months from receiving notice in writing from the Governor so to do, or if the lessee shall wholly discontinue operations under the lease during a continuous period of six months without the consent in writing of the Governor, then the lease may be determined by the Governor without prejudice to any claim against the lessee which shall already have accrued. The decision of the Governor determining the lease shall be sufficiently notified to the lessee by its publication in the Gazette, and shall operate to vest in the Government all the plant, buildings, and other property of the lessee in connection with the land leased without any payment or compensation to the lessee in respect thereof.

30. Any person who shall place or deposit, or be accessory to the placing or depositing of, any metal, ore, or mineral in any

spot or place for the purpose of misleading any person as to the nature, quality, or quantity of the mineral naturally occurring at such spot or place, or who shall mingle or cause to be mingled with any sample of metal, mineral, or ore, any valuable metal or any substance whatsoever which will increase the value or in any way change the nature of the said metal, mineral, or ore, with intention to defraud any person, shall be guilty of felony, and shall be liable, on conviction, to a penalty not exceeding £500 or to imprisonment for a term not exceeding five years.

31. There shall be kept at the principal office within the Protectorate of the lessee of a mining lease or his attorney (1) accurate and regular accounts containing full entries of all minerals raised or got under such lease, together with all such particulars as may be necessary to form an estimate of the quantity and value of such minerals; and (2) correct plans and sections of all mines worked under the rights conferred by his said lease, and of all the workings thereof, and of all veins or lodes which shall have been discovered therein, upon which the extent, position, and actual condition of the works shall at least once in every half year be accurately delineated. The scale of plans and sections shall be, for underground plans 1 in 500 and for surface plans 1 in 5000.

32. No officer, whether civil or military, shall, while in the service of the Government of the Protectorate, acquire or hold any right or interest under any prospecting right, licence to prospect, or mining lease, and any licence or lease purporting to confer any such right or interest on any such officer shall be null and void.

33. The Government Inspector of Mines may at any time enter and inspect any land over which an exclusive licence to

prospect or a mining lease has been granted, for the purpose of ascertaining the condition thereof, and may inspect and take copies of or extracts from any books or papers, plans, &c., dealing with the operations of the licensee or lessee, and required by this Proclamation to be kept.

34. The Governor shall have power to make rules and regulations for carrying this proclamation into effect and in particular for all or any of the following matters:—

(*a*) The manner in which applications for prospecting rights, exclusive licences to prospect, and mining leases shall be made, the forms to be used, and the fees payable in respect thereof;

(*b*) The information to be supplied by the applicants;

(*c*) The shape of areas over which exclusive licences to prospect may be granted and the manner in which the same shall be surveyed and beaconed;

(*d*) The manner in which the right of entry upon land shall be exercised; and the conditions on which shafts, pits, temporary buildings, and other works may be made or erected for the purpose of prospecting;

(*e*) The amount of work to be done under an exclusive licence to prospect;

(*f*) The construction of roads, tramways, and railways;

(*g*) The construction and erection of houses, machinery, and other works to be used for mining purposes;

(*h*) The fencing off or rendering secure of any of the works constructed, erected, or made for prospecting or mining purposes;

(*i*) The grazing of cattle and other animals, and the cutting down and use of timber for the purpose of carrying on prospecting operations;

(*k*) For securing the safety of persons employed in mines and for the carrying on of mining operations in a safe, proper, and effectual manner;

(*l*) The reference of disputes to a court for decision;

(*m*) The transfer and assignment of rights under licences and leases;

(*n*) The amount of royalty payable to the Government and the form and manner in which such royalty shall be collected and paid; and

(*o*) The grant of leases of the kinds numbered (3), (4), (5), and (6) in Section 17; and may attach to the breach of any such rule or regulation a penalty not exceeding £50 or imprisonment for a term not exceeding six months for each such breach.

Until further or other provision be made under this section, the rules and regulations set forth in the schedule hereto shall be and remain in force.

35. Nothing in this Proclamation shall be construed to refer to or to sanction the prospecting or mining for mineral oil of any kind.

36. Nothing in this Proclamation shall be construed to affect any rights existing at the date of its commencement.

THE SCHEDULE

Rules and Regulations

1.—(1) Any person desiring to obtain a prospecting right shall apply in writing for the same to the Governor through the Secretary to the Administration, and in making such application shall give the following particulars:—

> (*a*) The name, nationality, and description of the applicant, and an address in the Protectorate at which notices, &c., may be served;
>
> (*b*) The parts of the Protectorate in which the applicant desires to travel; and
>
> (*c*) A copy of the memorandum and articles of association of any syndicate or corporation on behalf of which the applicant is applying as aforesaid.

(2) The applicant shall show, if required by the Governor to do so, that he possesses sufficient money or credit to enable him to pay all reasonable travelling and prospecting expenses likely to be incurred in the exercise of the rights conferred by a prospecting right.

2. A prospecting right shall be in Form I. of the Appendix hereto.

3. The fee to be paid for a prospecting right shall be £5, and its duration shall be for one year from the granting of the right.

4. Any person desiring to obtain an exclusive licence to prospect may apply in writing to the Governor through the Secretary to the Administration, and in making such application shall give the following particulars:—

(*a*) The name, nationality, and description of the applicant, and if representing a corporation or company the like information with regard to the directors thereof, and the amount of cash, working capital, and nominal capital of such corporation or company, and an address in the Protectorate at which notices, &c., may be served;

(*b*) Copies of the memorandum and articles of association of any corporation, syndicate, or company represented by the applicant;

(*c*) The class, or combination of classes, of minerals for which the applicant desires to prospect; and

(*d*) The boundaries, area, and situation of the ground over which an exclusive licence is desired: Provided that

(1) The boundaries shall be defined in such a manner as to be a sufficient guide to others desiring to locate contiguous areas, and shall have been demarcated to the satisfaction of the Inspector of Mines;

(2) A sketch plan shall be furnished on the scale of 1:25,000, showing the topography and main drainage in such a manner as will illustrate the position of the boundaries and enable them to be identified upon the ground; and

(3) No statement of latitude and longitude shall be considered as defining an exclusive prospecting area.

5. Applications under the preceding regulation shall be submitted in duplicate, and one copy shall be filed in the office of the Secretary to the Administration (or at such other place as the Governor may appoint); and the file shall be open to inspection at all reasonable times.

6. The shape of an area over which an exclusive licence to prospect may be granted shall be such that the average width, as determined by dividing the area by the greatest length, is not less than one-third of the greatest length.

7. An exclusive licence to prospect shall be in Form II. of the Appendix hereto.

8. The fee to be paid for an exclusive licence to prospect shall be £5 per square mile or part of a square mile per annum.

9.—(1) The holder of an exclusive licence to prospect shall, under penalty of revocation of such licence under the provisions of section 11 of the Proclamation, during the whole of the period for which such licence is granted, either by himself or his agents, carry on *bonâ fide* prospecting operations.

(2) The Governor may refuse to renew any exclusive licence if satisfied that *bonâ fide* prospecting operations have not been carried on.

10. The holder of a prospecting right or an exclusive licence to prospect may in respect of the land subject to his right or licence exercise the following rights for the purpose of prospecting:—

> (*a*) Enter upon the said land unless the Governor shall by Government notice declare any part thereof to be closed to prospectors;
>
> (*b*) Erect temporary buildings or set up camp thereon;
>
> (*c*) Use any water thereon or divert any watercourse; provided that no stream of a greater width from bank to bank than 20 feet shall be diverted without the consent in writing of the Government Inspector of Mines;
>
> (*d*) Sink shafts or wells, or dig trenches; and

(*e*) Cut timber for any purpose essential to the work of carrying on prospecting operations in an efficient manner.

11. A prospecting right, an exclusive licence to prospect, and any licence granted under the provisions of the Proclamation or of these regulations, and a written authority given by the holder of an exclusive licence to any person to prospect upon his area, shall be produced to the Government Inspector of Mines demanding to inspect the same, and any person who shall fail to produce such licence, right, or authority when demanded as aforesaid shall be guilty of an offence and be liable to a penalty not exceeding £25.

12. An application for a mining lease shall be made through the Secretary to the Administration and shall contain the following particulars and information:—

(*a*) The name, nationality, and description of the applicant, and if a syndicate or corporation the like information with regard to the members or directors thereof, and the amount of the nominal and subscribed capital of such syndicate or corporation, and an address in the Protectorate at which notices, &c., may be served;

(*b*) A map on a scale of 1:5000 showing the boundaries, extent, and situation of the area in which it is desired to mine, and containing sufficient topographical information to enable the position of the area to be easily located;

(*c*) The length of term desired;

(*d*) Whether it is desired to dig for, mine, and work all

minerals and precious stones, or some one or more and which of them; and

(*e*) A copy of the memorandum and articles of association of any syndicate or corporation applying as aforesaid.

13. A mining lease shall be in the Form III., and an assignment thereof in the Form IV. set forth in the Appendix hereto, or as near thereto as circumstances admit.

14. All mining areas shall be bounded by straight lines and vertical planes from the surface boundary lines downwards to an unlimited depth from the surface.

13. Within a period not exceeding twelve months from the date of the commencement of a mining lease there shall be erected by the lessee beacons of a permanent character:—

(*a*) In the case of a lode mining lease, at the corners of each claim; and

(*b*) In the case of an alluvial lease, at each angular point of the polygon formed by the boundary lines, and at such other points as may be necessary to secure that no two consecutive beacons shall be more than 2000 feet apart: Provided that where for any reason it may be impracticable to comply strictly with these provisions, the Government Inspector of Mines may authorise the placing of beacons at such other points as may in his opinion most conveniently define the boundaries of the area.

16. A lessee of a mining lease shall keep his beacons and boundary marks in good condition and repair so that they shall be at all times a reasonable guide for persons desirous of marking out contiguous areas.

17. The lessee of a mining lease shall within twelve months of date of granting of such lease, or within such further time as the Governor by writing under his hand may grant, commence mining operations upon the lands subject to his said lease.

18. The lessee of a mining lease will at all times during the continuance thereof, except during the first twelve months, and unless prevented by any disturbances, or by unavoidable accident, effectually and vigorously work and develop and carry on mining operations on the land subject to the said lease.

19. No mine shall be considered to be effectually or properly worked within the meaning of the preceding regulation unless it can be shown that an expenditure per annum has been incurred in respect of working on the ground of at least £2 per acre in the case of an alluvial, and £100 per claim in the case of a lode mining, lease.

Provided that in the case of contiguous leases held by the same person or corporation, the Governor may, on cause being shown, allow any two or more of the said leases to be regarded as one for the purpose of calculating the expenditure required by this regulation.

20. In any case where tailings or any other products whatever from the operations of mining or metallurgy are being discharged, or about to be discharged, in such a manner as to hinder or injuriously affect any other person in the execution of his legal mining rights, or the future development of mining, it shall be lawful for the Government Inspector of Mines to order the disposal of such products or tailings in some other manner not detrimental to present or future mining.

21. It shall not be lawful for any person to construct under-ground any magazine for the storage of explosives, or to erect

a magazine for such purpose upon the surface of the ground without previously having obtained permission in writing from the Government Inspector of Mines. Any such magazine shall be erected subject to the following conditions:—

(*a*) It shall be constructed at a distance of at least 100 yards from any occupied building, public road, bridge, aqueduct, or railway, or structure that might sustain damage in the event of an explosion;

(*b*) The walls shall be of suitable and substantial construction;

(*c*) The roof shall be as light as possible, but fire-proof;

(*d*) It shall be provided with a reliable lightning conductor, which shall have its lower end attached to a metal plate at least four square feet in area which shall be buried at least three feet in the ground, and the point at which the conductor enters the ground, and the ground in which it is buried, shall be as far as possible kept damp;

(*e*) It shall have no windows;

(*f*) The door shall be provided with a stout lock and be kept fastened when not in use;

(*g*) The ground within a radius of sixty yards shall be kept clear of bushes and grass.

22. On or before the 8th of each month, or as soon after as circumstances will permit, every manager or person in charge of mining operations shall lodge with the Government Inspector of Mines a written statement setting forth:—

(1) The name and designation of the property;

(2) The name of the owners of the mine;

(3) The nature of the mine;

(4) The output of mineral in the preceding month;

(5) A statement of working costs;

(6) The number of employees and labourers in the preceding month, and the total amount of wages paid to the labourers and the total amount of salaries of Europeans that are a charge on the mine, including those on leave;

(7) The particulars of any deaths or accidents that may have occurred during the preceding month; and

(8) Any further particulars that may be required by the Government Inspector of Mines for the purpose of compiling statistics.

23.—(1) There shall be payable to the Government by all lessees of mining leases a royalty of £5 per centum upon the value of all metal won.

(2) If such metal or any ore containing metal be exported from the Protectorate, such royalty shall be collected in the form of an export duty payable upon exportation at any customs station in the Protectorate.

(3) The value of such metal shall be deemed to be the actual market price of the metal in the London market on the 1st day of January, April, July, or October next preceding the exportation.

(4) The value of tin ore shall be deemed to be at the rate of 70 per centum of the value of metallic tin computed as aforesaid.

24. Any person wilfully committing a breach of these regulations or refusing to obey an order lawfully given under any of the provisions thereof shall in addition to any liability to

forfeiture provided by the Proclamation be liable to a penalty not exceeding £50, or in default to imprisonment for a term not exceeding six months.

APPENDIX

FORM I.

The Minerals Proclamation, 1910 (Northern Nigeria).

Prospecting Right ____, No. ____.

Licence, subject to the provisions of the said Proclamation and of the rules and regulations made thereunder, is hereby granted for twelve months from the date hereof to E. F. [*here insert name, address, and description of licensee]* to prospect for minerals [*or as the case may be*] in such parts of the Protectorate as may not from time to time be closed to prospectors by Government Notice in the Gazette.

This ____ day of ____ 19____

(Signed) GOVERNOR.

FORM II.

The Minerals Proclamation, 1910 (Northern Nigeria), Exclusive Licence to Prospect. No. ____.

The exclusive right, subject to the provisions of the said Proclamation, and of the rules and regulations made thereunder, for one year from the ____ day of ____ is hereby granted to A. B. [*here insert name, address, and description of licensee*] to prospect for minerals [*or as the case may be*] within the following limits [*here insert boundaries of area*] as the same are delineated on the map attached hereto and coloured.

This ____ day of ____ 19____

(Signed) Governor.

FORM III.

The Minerals Proclamation, 1910 (Northern Nigeria), Mining Lease.

This lease is granted to ____ of ____ for mining purposes upon or under [*here describe area with boundaries*] as the same is delineated on the map attached hereto for the period of ____ years from the date hereof according to the true intent and meaning of the said Proclamation and subject to the provisions of the said Proclamation or of any Proclamation amending, altering, or repealing the same, and to all such rules and regulations as may from time to time be made under such Proclamation or Proclamations.

Dated this ____ day of ____ 19 ____

(Signed) Governor.

FORM IV.

The Minerals Proclamation, 1910 (Northern Nigeria),
Assignment of Mining Lease.

Whereas under the provisions of the above-mentioned Proclamation a lease for mining purposes upon or under [*here describe area with boundaries, &c., as in original lease*] was on the ____ day of ____ 19____, granted to ____ of ____ for a term of ____ years from the date thereof, and duly registered in Vol.

_____ page _____ of the register of instruments affecting land. Now these presents witness that in consideration of the sum of _____ the said _____ [*lessee*] doth hereby assign to _____ of _____ all his right title and interest in and under the said lease as from the _____ day of _____ for the remainder of the term thereof.

In witness, &c.

1 PART OF MARINA, LAGOS, SOUTHERN NIGERIA

2 MARINA, SHOWING CUSTOMS, LAGOS, SOUTHERN NIGERIA

3 LAGOS

4 LAGOS. AMONGST THE PALMS

5 BIRD'S-EYE VIEW SHOWING MARINA AND TOWN, LAGOS

6 A PORTION OF LAGOS TOWN FROM ROOF OF NEW MOSQUE

7 LAGOS

8 WEST END OF LAGOS FROM THE FRENCH FACTORY

9 STEAM TRAM, MARINA, LAGOS

10 LAGOS

11 BUSINESS PREMISES, MARINA, LAGOS

12 PART OF MARINA, LAGOS

13 THE MARINA, LAGOS

14 CLUB-HOUSE, LAGOS

15 POST OFFICE, LAGOS

16 GOVERNMENT HOUSE, LAGOS

17 PUBLIC WASH "HOUSES," LAGOS

18 PUBLIC WASHING PLACE, ELEGRATA, LAGOS

19 RAILWAY, IDDO

20 YAMS (POTATOES) ON THE BEACH, LAGOS

21 FRUIT MARKET, LAGOS

22 CORNER OF MARKET, LAGOS

23 IDDO STATION, LAGOS

24 RAILWAY ENGINE, IDDO

25 FULANI SHEEP, LAGOS

26 BULLOCK CART

27 FORCADOS, SOUTHERN NIGERIA

28 "SIR ALFRED" DRY DOCK, FORCADOS

29 BOTANICAL GARDENS, EBUTE METTA, LAGOS

30 BOTANICAL GARDENS, EBUTE METTA, LAGOS

31 RAILWAY CROSSING, EBUTE METTA, LAGOS

32 ON THE ROAD TO EBUTE METTA, LAGOS

33 THE MARKET, BURUTU, SOUTHERN NIGERIA

34 BURUTU MARKET

35 GOVERNMENT BOAT AT BURUTU

36 PALM OIL STORES, BURUTU

37 HOSPITAL, BURUTU

38 KWA RIVER, CALABAR. MOTOR BOAT "SPIDER," DRAUGHT 9 INCHES

39 TWO JAKRIE WOMEN, BURUTU, SOUTHERN NIGERIA

40 JAKRIE CHIEF AND ONE OF HIS WIVES

41 LARGE "COTTON TREE" AT OKUNI, CROSS RIVER

42 JAKRIE WOMAN, BURUTU

43 CHIEF OKRODODO AND TWO OF HIS SONS, BURUTU

44 CHIEF OKRODODO, HIS SONS AND DAUGHTERS: JAKRIE
TRIBE, BURUTU

45 NATIVE DANCERS AT AWKA IN THE ONITSHA HINTERLAND
BETWEEN NIGER AND THE CROSS RIVER

46 NATIVE MARKET AT ITU ON CROSS RIVER

47 A LANDING PLACE ON CROSS RIVER

48 ON THE EWAYONG, A TRIBUTARY OF THE CROSS RIVER

49 A BRIDGE OVER AUJA RIVER NEAR OGOJA

50 BRIDGE BUILT OF VINES BY PAGANS

51 THE "SPIDER" AT ITU

52 OSHOGBO RAILWAY STATION: LADY EGERTON AND DISTRICT
COMMISSIONER, MR. GLADSTONE, IN FOREGROUND

53 COCOANUT AND BANANA PALMS

54 SIR WALTER EGERTON, LADY EGERTON, CAPT. LAWRENCE,
PRIVATE SECRETARY, CAPT. LLOYD, A.D.C.

55 LOWER NIGER

56 LOWER NIGER

57 ON THE BANKS OF THE LOWER NIGER

58 SHIPPING RUBBER, LOWER NIGER

59 VILLAGE ON THE LOWER NIGER

60 IDAH, RIVER NIGER

61 MESSRS. G. W. CHRISTIAN'S STORE AT IDAH, NIGER RIVER

62 EJAWS: VILLAGE SCENE, LOWER NIGER

63 BRIDGE OF SIGHS, LOKOJA, NORTHERN NIGERIA

64 MAIN STREET, LOKOJA MARKET

65 NATIVE JUDGE OR ALKALE AT LOKOJA (COPY OF THE KORAN
ON HIS LAP)

66 ASABA BOYS, SOUTHERN NIGERIA

67 "BOYS" WHO WORK THE CARGO

68 SHIPPING COTTON, LOKOJA, NORTHERN NIGERIA

69 NIGER COMPANY'S DEPOT AT LOKOJA

70 PRODUCE STORES, LOKOJA

71 LOKOJA MARKET

72 LOKOJA MARKET

73 LOKOJA MARKET

74 LOKOJA MARKET

75 YAMS ON THE BEACH, LOKOJA

76 AT THE RIVER-SIDE, LOKOJA

77 LOKOJA

78 LOKOJA

79 MARINE BUNGALOW, LOKOJA

80 EUROPEAN HOSPITAL, LOKOJA

81 CANTEEN AT LOKOJA

82 BANK, LOKOJA

83 KING ABIGA, LOKOJA, NORTHERN NIGERIA

84 DEVIL MAN, LOKOJA

85 LOKOJA

86 LOKOJA

87 CAMP ROAD, LOKOJA

88 CAMP ROAD, LOKOJA

89 BARRACKS, LOKOJA

90 THE SERRIKIN (KING OF LOKOJA) AND HIS CHIEFS AT THE
KING'S HOUSE

91 MEAT-MARKET. LOKOJA

92 GUARD ON GOVERNMENT TREASURY. LOKOJA

93 MESSRS. CHRISTIAN'S STORE, LOKOJA

94 HAUSAS LOVE SOAP AND WATER

95 COMING IN FROM THE COUNTRY, LOKOJA

96 LOKOJA

97 BRIDGE OF SIGHS, LOKOJA

98 GOVERNMENT OFFICIALS AND OTHERS WATCHING GYMKANA, LOKOJA

99 HAUSA WOMEN HAIRDRESSING, LOKOJA, NORTHERN NIGERIA

100 BARBERS, LOKOJA MARKET

101 NATIVE BARBER

102 PREPARING FOOFOO (CRUSHED YAMS), LOKOJA

103 CHILDREN AT PLAY, LOKOJA

104 CHILDREN IN THE MARKET, LOKOJA, NORTHERN NIGERIA

105 WASHING UP, RIVER NIGER

106 A QUARREL, LOKOJA MARKET

107 WASHING DAY ON THE NIGER RIVER, NORTHERN NIGERIA

108 NATIVE TRADING CANOE, UPPER NIGER, NORTHERN
NIGERIA

109 GROUP OF HAUSA AND NUPE CHIEFS (SERRIKIN OF LOKOJA
IN CENTRE)

110 BLACK BLUEJACKETS ON THE GOVERNMENT RIVER
STEAMER "KAPELLI"

111 S.W. "NDONI" (CARGO BOAT) ON THE RIVER NIGER

112 "HALSTEAD" (CARGO BOAT) ON NIGER RIVER

113 HIGH COMMISSIONER'S YACHT "CORONA" ON THE NIGER

114 HAUSA CANOE

115 CHIEF'S CANOE BEING SALUTED ON THE NIGER

116 NUPE TOWN OF EGGA ON THE NIGER

117 EGGA, NORTHERN NIGERIA

118 EGBOHU, NORTHERN NIGERIA, LANDING PLACE OF
EXPEDITION AGAINST BEDA

119 PART OF RABBA VILLAGE, NORTHERN NIGERIA

120 UNLOADING SALT, JEBBA

121 LOADING STEAMER, JEBBA

122 THE "S.S. SCARBOROUGH" AT JEBBA

123 LOOKING UP THE NIGER FROM JEBBA

124 MOHAMMEDAN MOSQUE, NORTHERN NIGERIA

125 PALM VILLAGE, NORTHERN NIGERIA

126 SHONGA, NORTHERN NIGERIA
B.C.G.A. have a ginnery here

127 FULANI CATTLE, NORTHERN NIGERIA

128 ON THE BENUE RIVER

129 CAMPING ON BENUE RIVER

130 MARKET AT LAMUGO, NEAR KEFFI

131 COWRIE MEN PAYING CARRIERS PER BASKET

132 MAKING LAMA MATS

133 MAKING STOOLS

134 GRINDING GUINEA CORN

135 JUKUMS AT ABINSI

136 THE EMIR OF KANO
(Now a prisoner in Lokoja. Was the cause of the Kano rising in 1907)

137 THREE HAUSA TRADERS WITH BUNDLES OF SKINS FROM
KANO

138 CATTLE, NEAR NAFADA

139 CAMELS AT NAFADA

140 SELLING COTTON IN NAFADA MARKET

141 CHIEF OF KANAM

142 HEAD MEN IN VOM

143 MIANGO CHIEF AND HEAD MEN (EX-CHIEF ON LEFT)

144 CHIEF OF WASE

145 CAMPS IN HOS

146 HAUSA LOOM

147 SECOND CHIEF AT IBI

148 WASE ROCK

149 AMO MEN

150 HAUSA GIRL

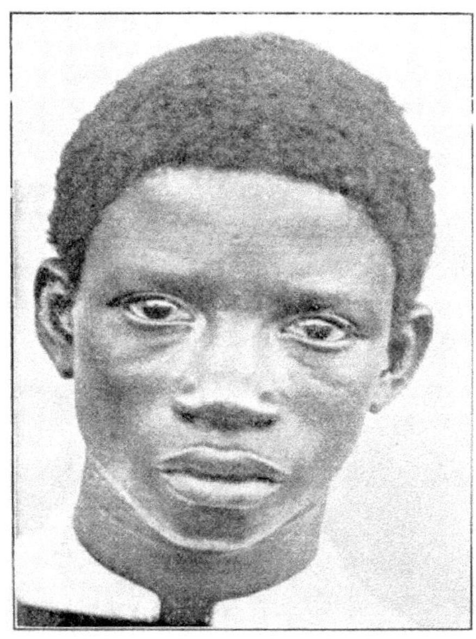

151 KABBA BOY

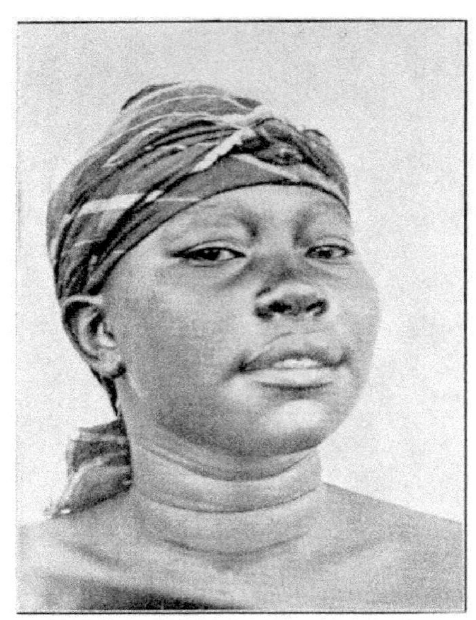

152 HAUSA WOMAN

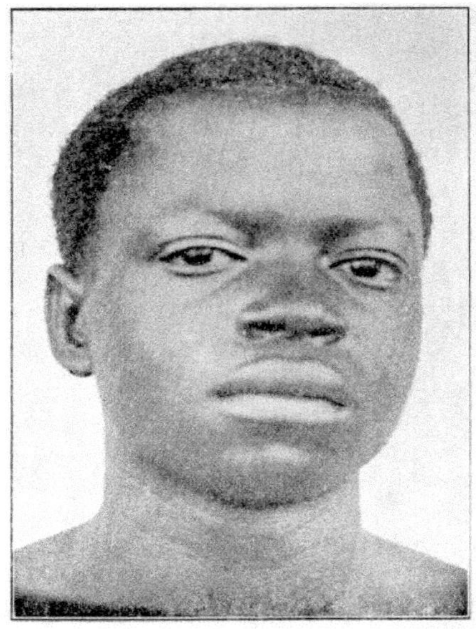

153 HAUSA BOY

154 BROTHER HEALY AND SOME OF HIS PUPILS, ONITSHA

155 VIEW ON THE RIVER NIGER

156 MESSRS. G. W. CHRISTIAN'S STORE, ONITSHA

157 SIR WILLIAM WALLACE, K.C.M.G

158 MR. S. R. BASTARD
(Chairman Champion Gold Reefs of West Africa, Ltd., and other important Nigerian Companies)

159 MR. LAWS IN FRONT OF OFFICE WITH BARS OF TIN READY FOR TRANSPORT

160 FIRST CAMP AT THE TIN MINES, NARAGUTA

161 NARAGUTA CAMP

162 PART OF THE FUEL MARKET, BAUCHI

163 SURVEYING PARTY AT JUGA

164 PAGANS PAYING A VISIT TO DISCUSS MATTERS AT JOS

165 PAGANS BRINGING IN A PRESENT, JOS

166 NARAGUTA. PAGANS COMING IN FOR TIN LOADS TO JERMAAN (We were fighting them a year before)

167 CARRIERS LEAVING NARAGUTA CAMP

168 CARRIERS CROSSING DELIMI RIVER

169 NARAGUTA. 190 BARS OF TIN LEAVING CAMP BY ASAB PAGANS

170 A CAMP. SURVEY CAMP AT JOS

171 HORSES BEING BROUGHT AS TAX

172 PART OF ACTUAL WORKING FACE, NARAGUTA

173 LAUNDERS AT END OF TAIL RACE AT RIVER'S EDGE, NARAGUTA

174 NARAGUTA. MAKING DAM

175 NARAGUTA. CONSTRUCTION OF DAM. RUKUBAR PAGANS

176 NARAGUTA. VIEW SHOWING BACK OF DAM

177 NARAGUTA DAM

178 NARAGUTA

179 NARAGUTA

180 NARAGUTA

181 NARAGUTA. FOUR SLUICE-BOXES IN LABOURERS' CREEK

182 NARAGUTA

183 NARAGUTA. VIEW OF SLUICE-BOXES, LABOURERS' CREEK

184 NARAGUTA. MOVING BOXES TO FACE OF STOPE,
BALA'S STOPE

185 NARAGUTA. TWO SLUICE-BOXES

186 NARAGUTA

187 NARAGUTA

188 NARAGUTA CAMP

189 OPENING FOOT-BRIDGE, DELIMI RIVER, NARAGUTA

190 LABOURERS' CAMP ON THE TIN FIELDS

191 NARAGUTA. TIN-WORKERS WORKING THE BED OF THE
RIVER IN DRY SEASON

192 NARAGUTA. CONSTRUCTION OF LEAT
BY RUKUBAR PAGANS

193 NARAGUTA. CONSTRUCTION OF LEAT
BY RUKUBAR PAGANS

194 WASHING TIN IN DELIMI RIVER, NARAGUTA

195 DELIMI RIVER

196 VIEW OF DELIMI RIVER BETWEEN NARAGUTA AND JOS

197 NARAGUTA. VIEW SHOWING FLOOD-BOXES ON LEAT

198 NARAGUTA

199 A CAMP

200 NARAGUTA. TRIBUTERS WASHING TIN

201 TIN WASHING

202 NARAGUTA. HALF-LENGTH NEW MAIN TAIL RACE

203 NARAGUTA. NO. 2. LOOKING UP MAIN TAIL RACE

204 NARAGUTA. LOWER VIEW, NO. 2, MAIN TAIL RACE

205 NARAGUTA. CLOSE TO MAIN WORKING FACE, NO. 2 STOPE

206 NARAGUTA. TIN MINING. YORUBUS WORKING IN
THE GROUND

207 TROOPS LEAVING NARAGUTA CAMP FOR BAUCHI

208 NAFUTA GORGE, LOOKING TOWARDS JUGA
The Juga River runs down the centre and passes to the Nafuta Flats

209 NAFUTA GORGE
The river at this point is lost to sight thirty feet below the big boulders in the middle of the ravine

210 PROPOSED DAM SITE, JUGA

211 PROSPECTING ON DUBBO OR TOPAZ VALLEY

212 MR. C. G. LUSH'S CAMP AT JUGA

213 CAMP OF MESSRS. LUSH, HUDDART, AND WALTER
WETHERED

214 MESSRS. HUDDART AND LUSH PROSPECTING ON ONE OF
THE CREEKS OF THE DUBBO OR TOPAZ VALLEY PROPERTY

215 FACE OF ALLUVIAL, 16 FEET DEEP, AVERAGING ABOUT 6
LBS. OF TIN PER CUBIC YARD: DUBBO OR TOPAZ VALLEY MINE

216 JUGA CAMP: PAY-DAY

217 RAFINSIROMA CAMP

218 RAFINSIROMA DAM, LOOKING SOUTH-EAST

219 HOUSE-BUILDING, RAFINSIROMA TIN MINES

220 A GROUP OF NATIVES

221 VIEW IN AMO

222 A VIEW IN VOM

223 MR. G. W. CHRISTIAN
A Nigerian Trader

224 STEAMERS DISCHARGING AT BARO

225 BARO RAILWAY YARD

226 BARO BEACH JUST BEFORE THE RAILWAY WAS BEGUN: BARO-KANO RAILWAY

227 SETTING OUT EARTHWORK AT PATATIFI, BARO-KANO LINE

228 TEMPORARY BRIDGE OVER THE BAKOGI RIVER,
BARO-KANO LINE

229 ENGINE OF THE EMIR CLASS ON STEEL BRIDGE,
BARO-KANO LINE

230 EARTHWORK IN PROGRESS, BARO-KANO LINE

231 STRAIGHTENING ROAD AT RAILHEAD, BARO-KANO LINE

232 NIGER END OF THE LINE: VIEW FROM BARO HILL

233 GENERAL VIEW OF BARO STATION

234 MR. H. W. LAWS
Engineer to the Niger Company

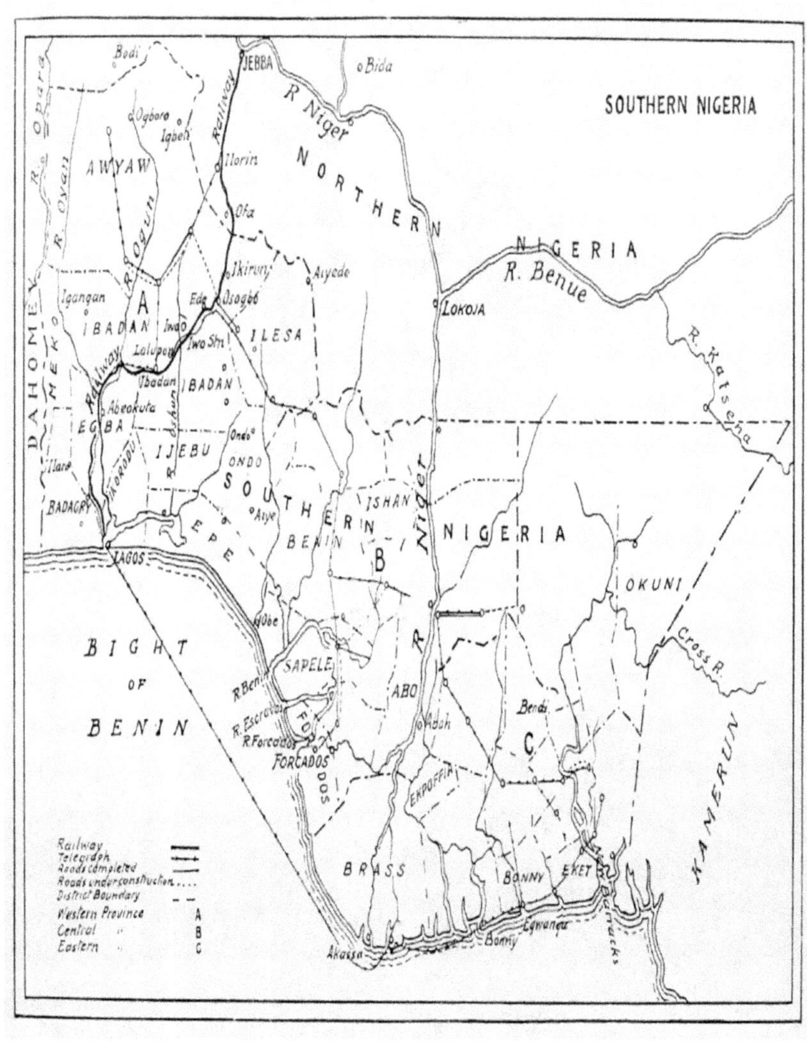

235 MAP OF SOUTHERN NIGERIA

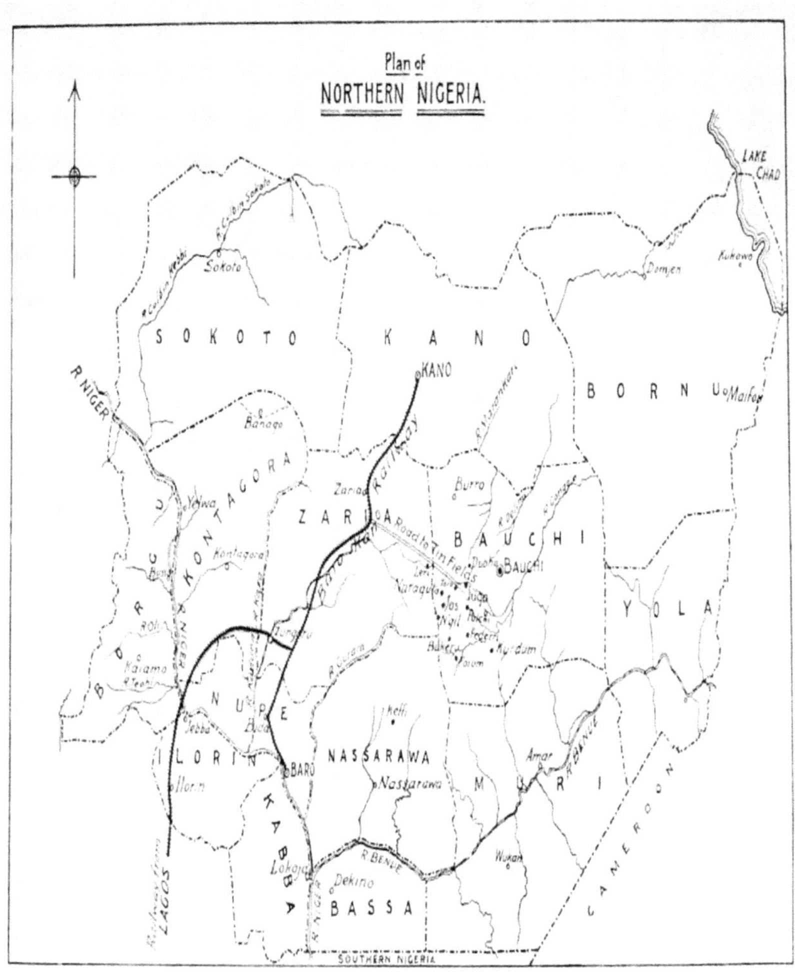

236 MAP OF NORTHERN NIGERIA

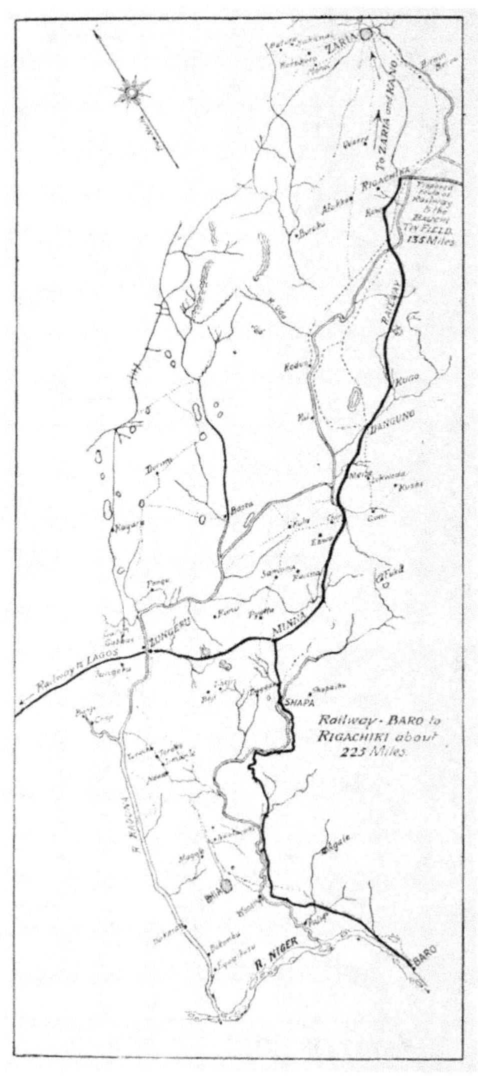

237 MAP SHOWING ROUTE OF RAILWAY FROM BARO TO RIGACHIKA, ABOUT 225 MILES

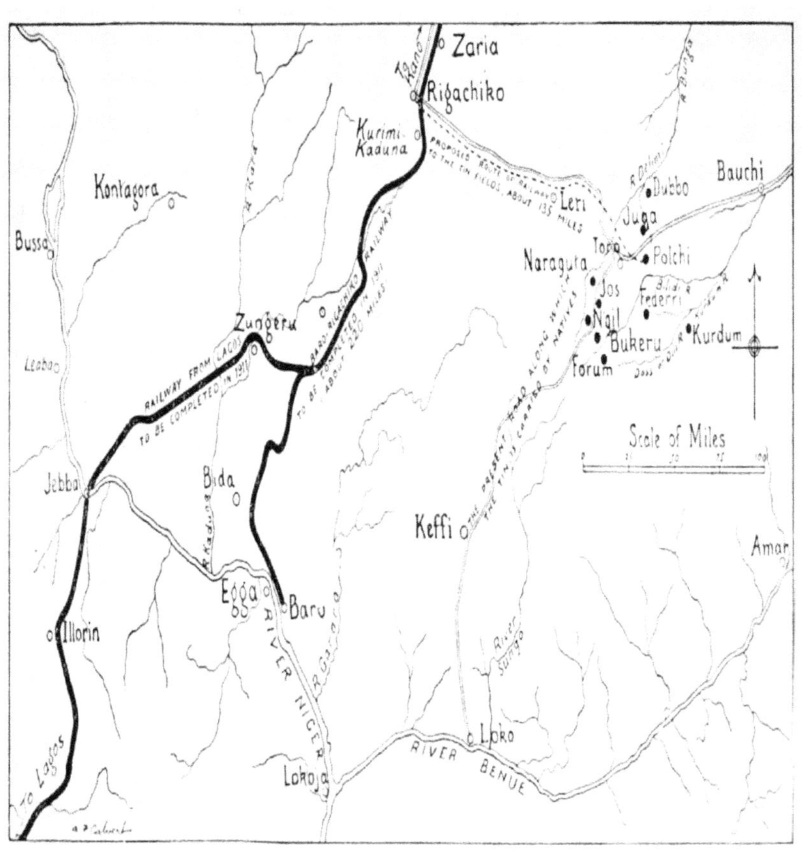

238 MAP SHOWING RAILWAY AND ROADS TO
THE BAUCHI TIN FIELDS

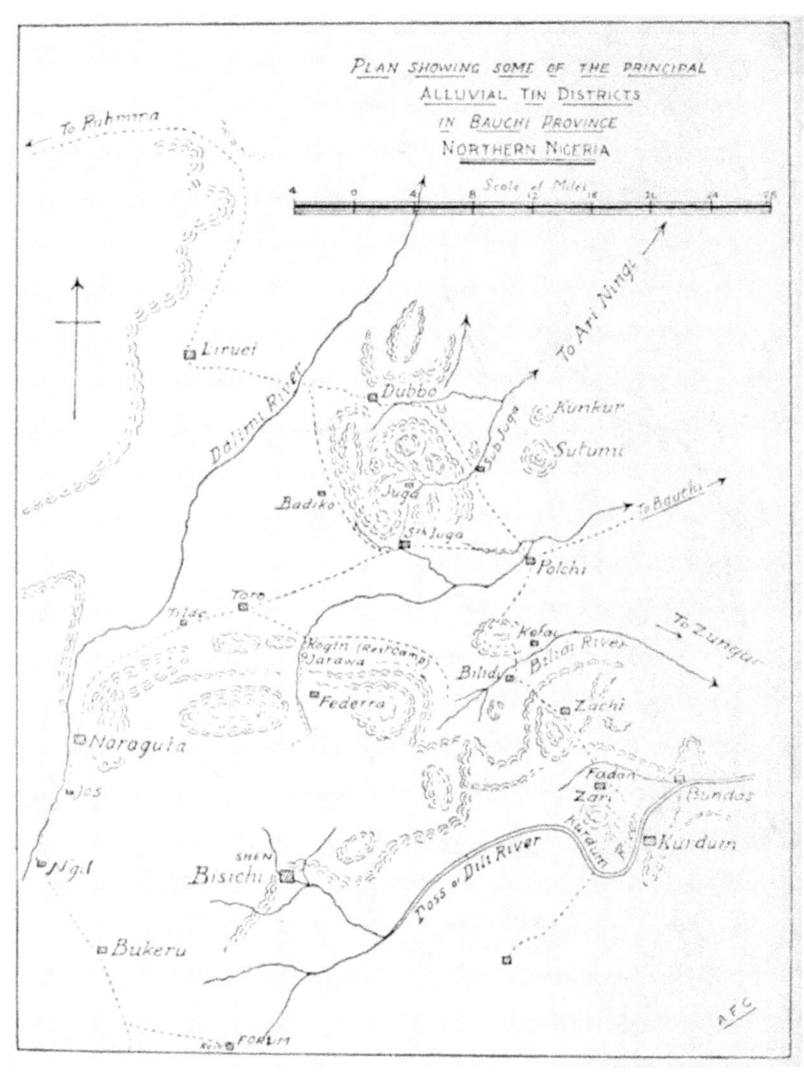

239 ALLUVIAL TIN DISTRICTS IN THE BAUCHI PROVINCE

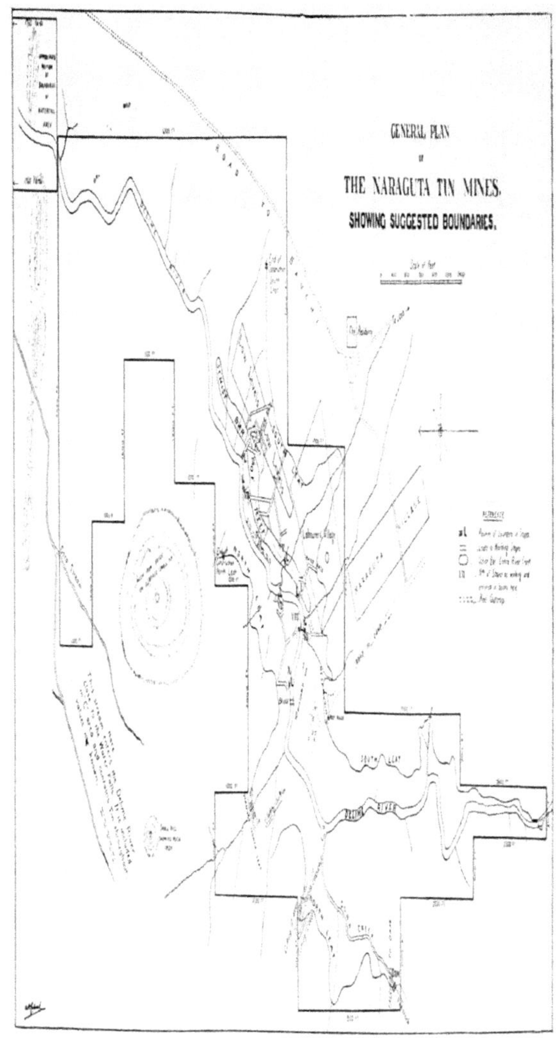

240 PLAN OF THE NARAGUTA TIN MINES SHOWING WORKINGS

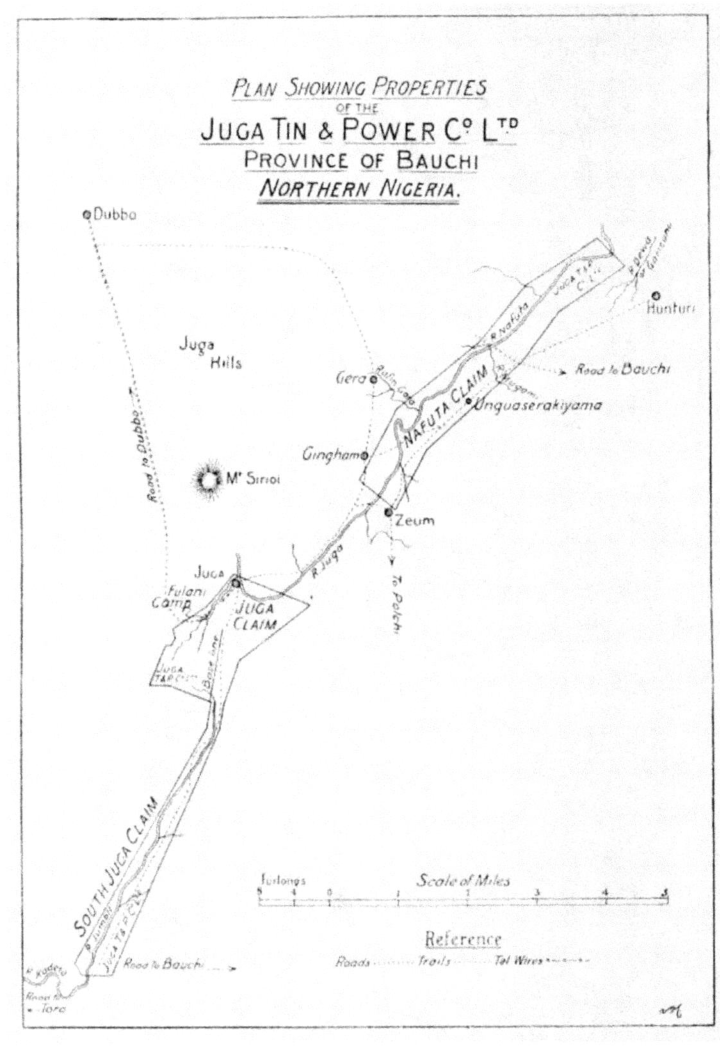

241 PROPERTIES OF THE JUGA (NIGERIA) TIN AND POWER CO.
LTD.

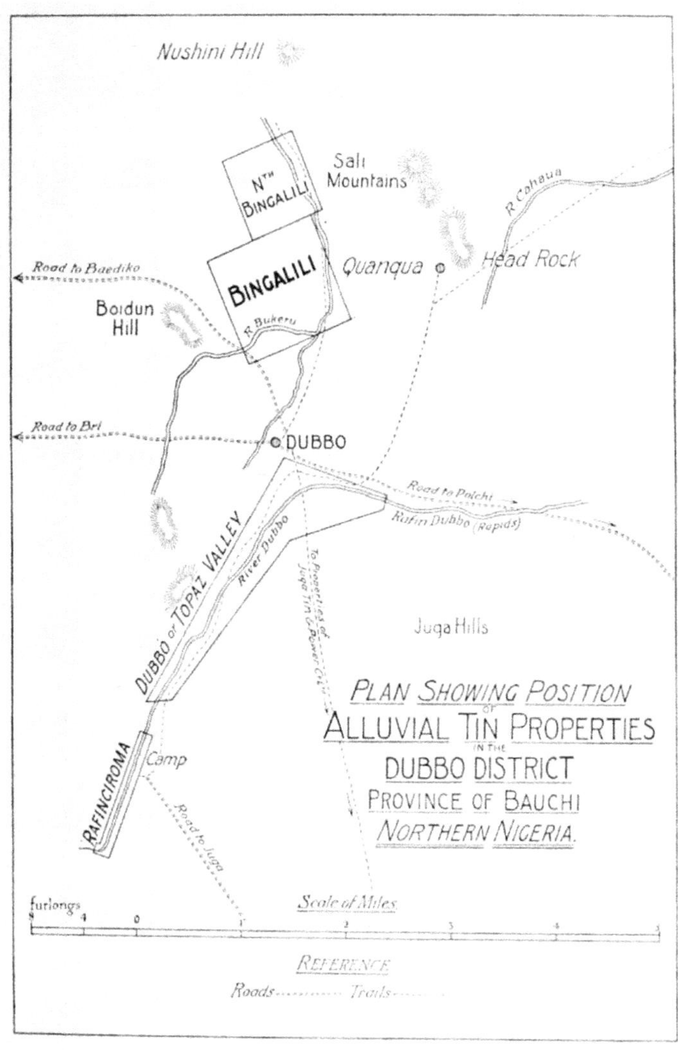

242 PROPERTIES OF THE LUCKY CHANCE MINES, LTD., IN THE
DUBBO DISTRICT

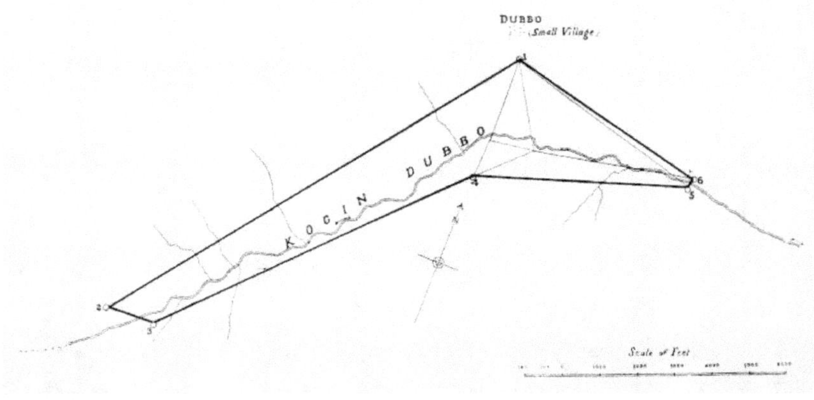

243 THE DUBBO OR TOPAZ VALLEY PROPERTY
Belonging to the Lucky Chance Mines, Limited

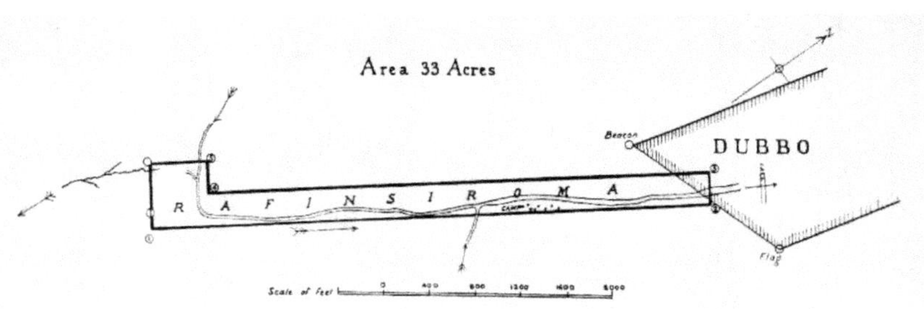

244 RAFINSIROMA TIN PROPERTY
Belonging to the Lucky Chance Mines, Limited

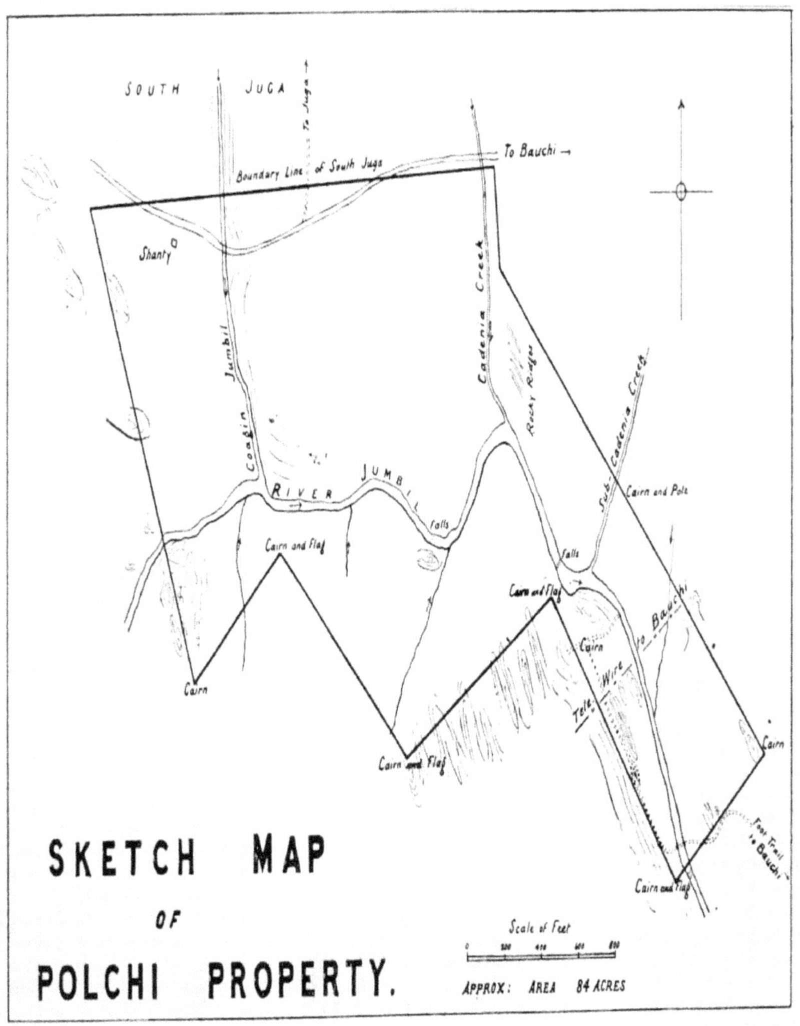

245 THE POLCHI ALLUVIAL TIN PROPERTY
Belonging to the Lucky Chance Mines, Limited

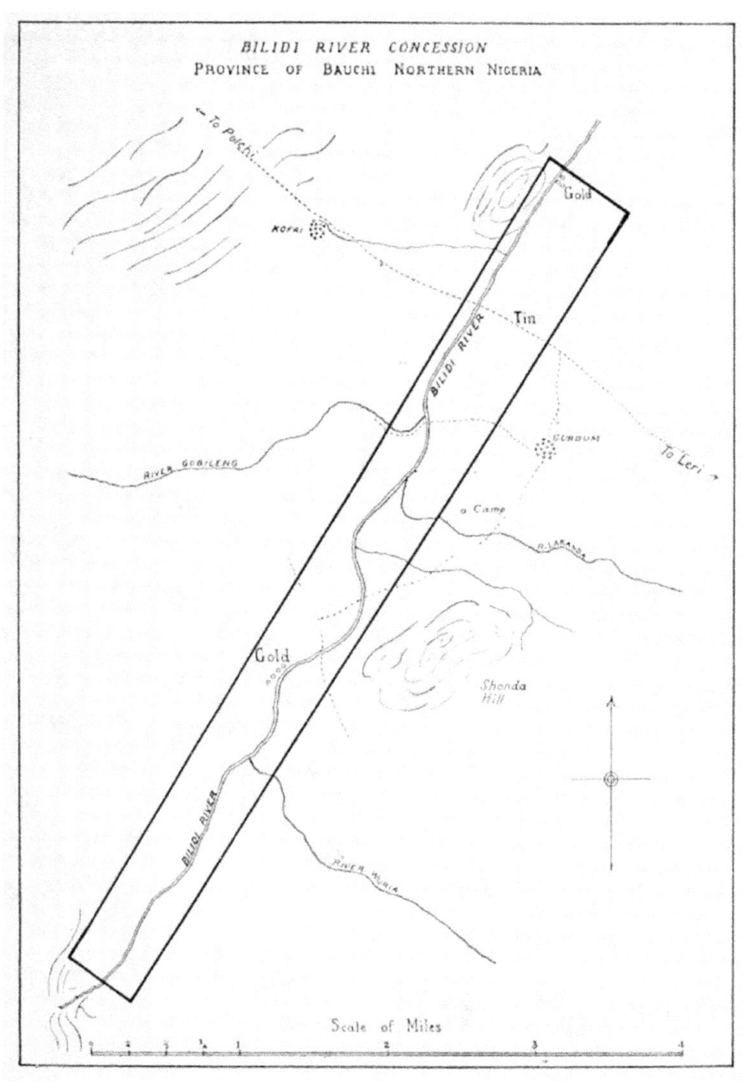

246 THE BILIDI ALLUVIAL TIN PROPERTY
Belonging to the Lucky Chance Mines, Limited

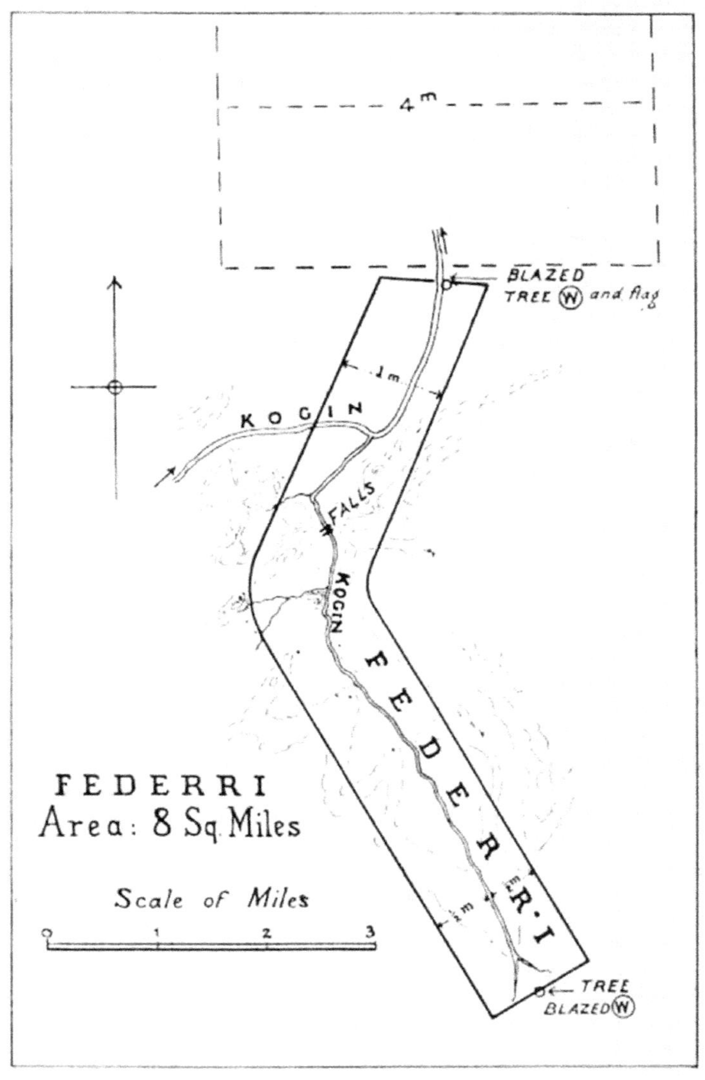

247 THE FEDERRI ALLUVIAL TIN PROPERTY
Tin Fields of Northern Nigeria, Limited

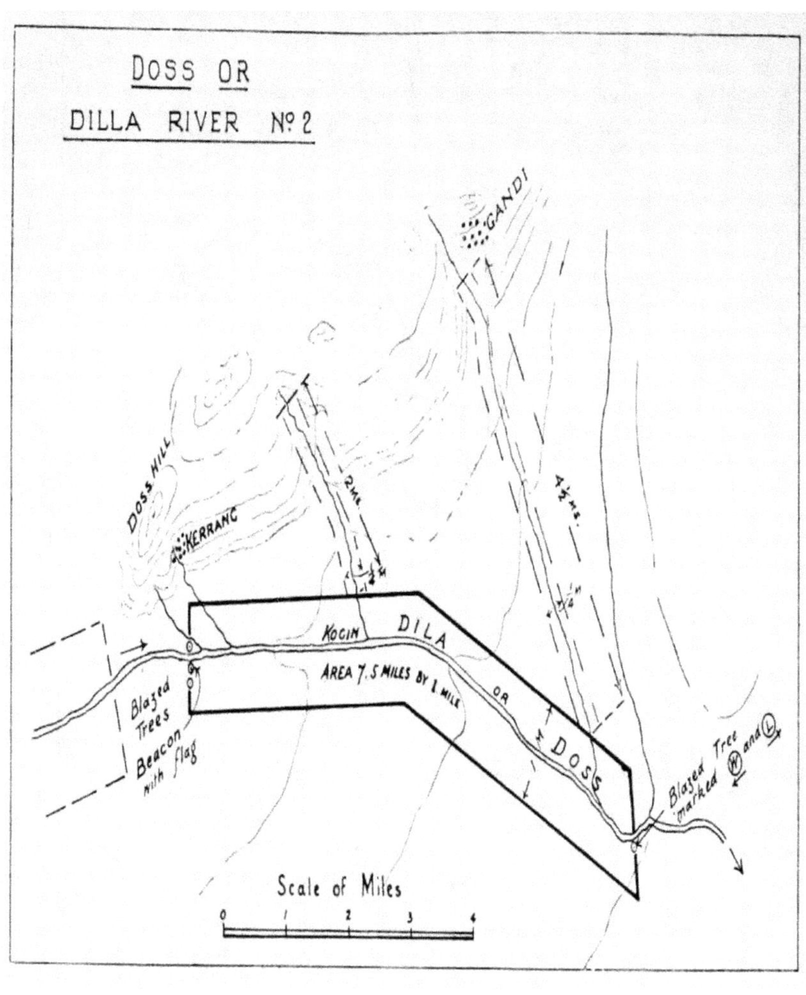

248 DOSS OR DILA TIN PROPERTY
Tin Fields of Northern Nigeria, Limited

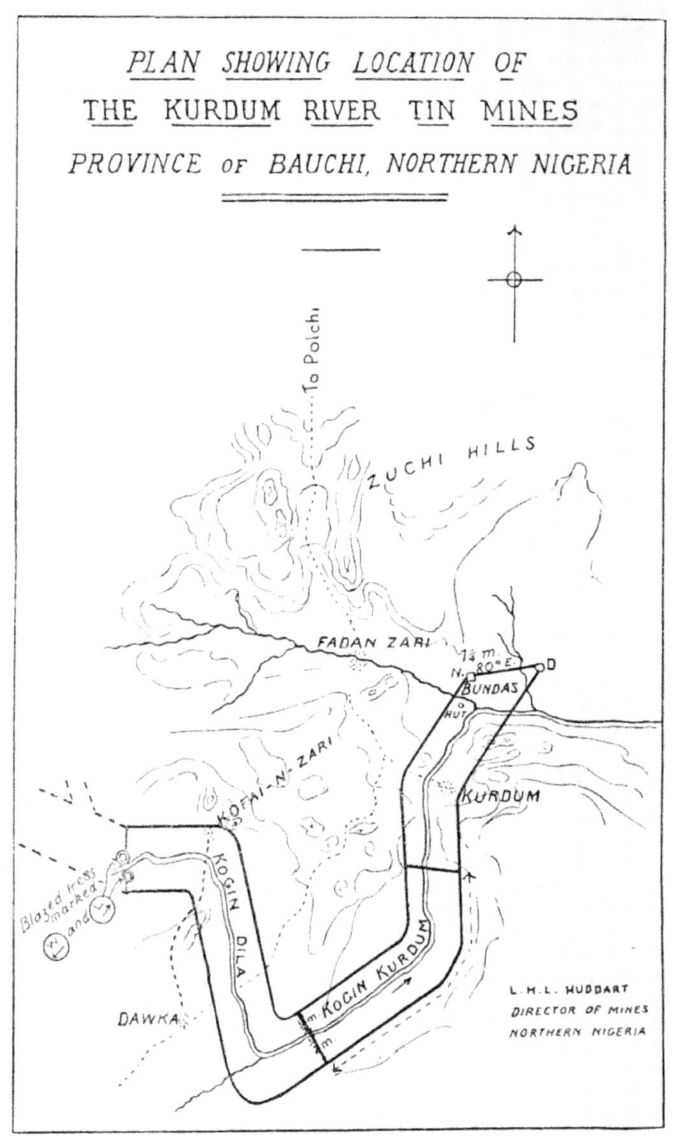

249 KURDUM RIVER ALLUVIAL TIN AREA

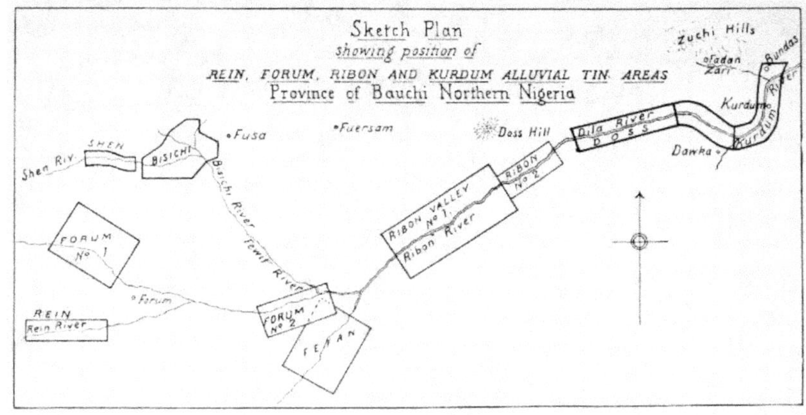

250 REIN, FORUM, RIBON AND KURDUM ALLUVIAL TIN AREAS

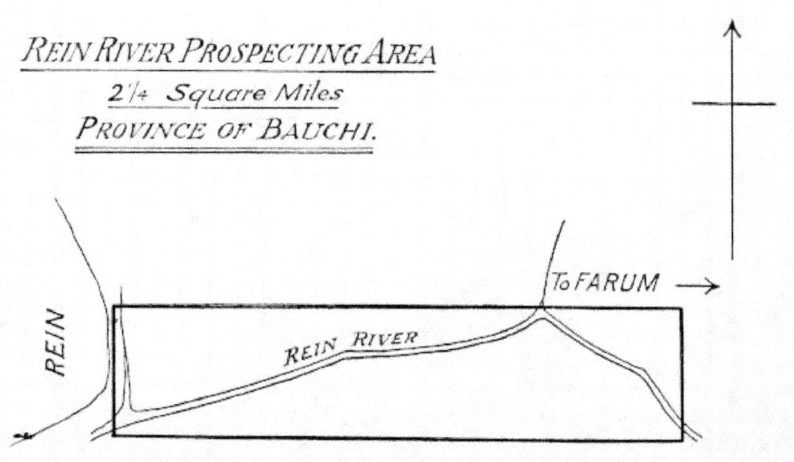

251 REIN ALLUVIAL TIN AREA
Rein River (Nigeria), Tin Mining Co.

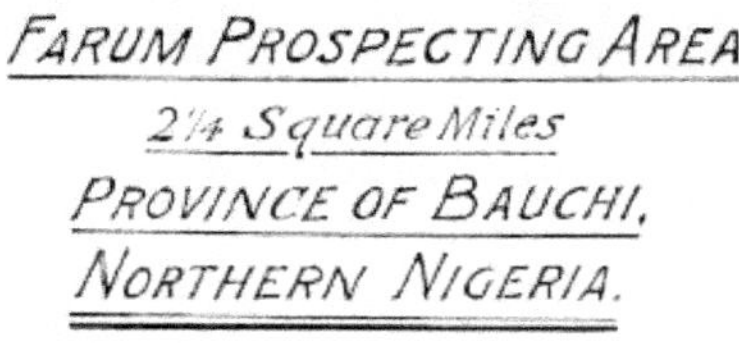

252 FARUM ALLUVIAL TIN AREA

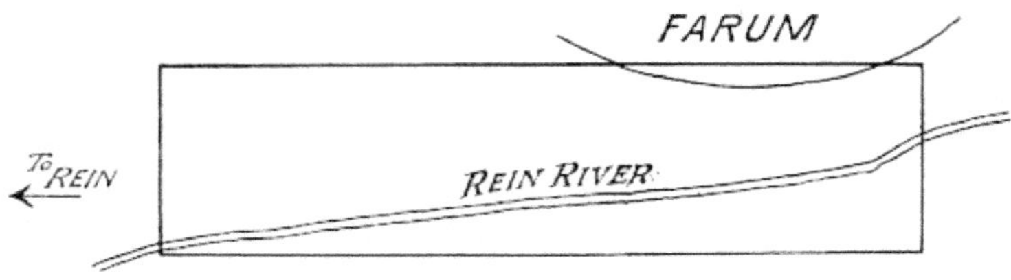
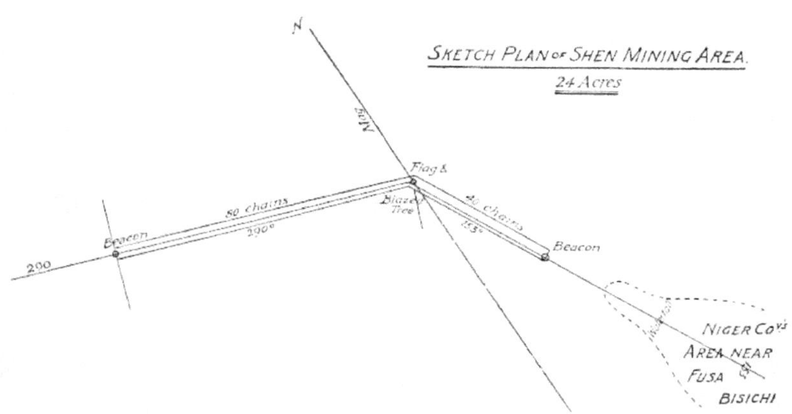

253 SHEN ALLUVIAL TIN AREA

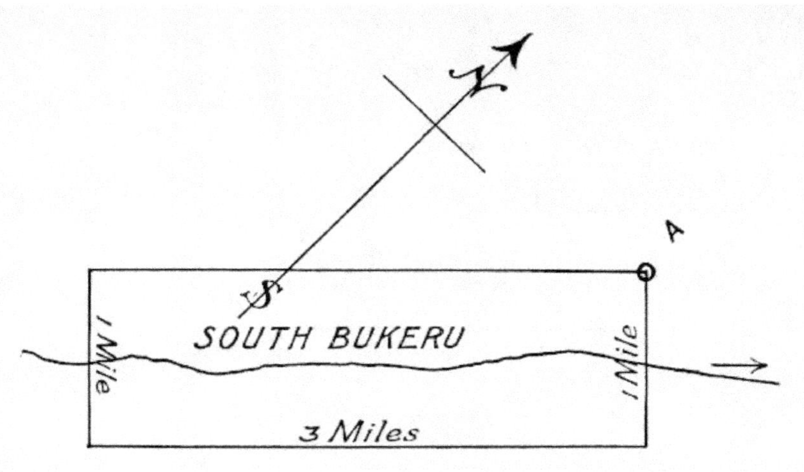

254 SOUTH BUKERU (NIGERIA) TIN MINES, LTD.

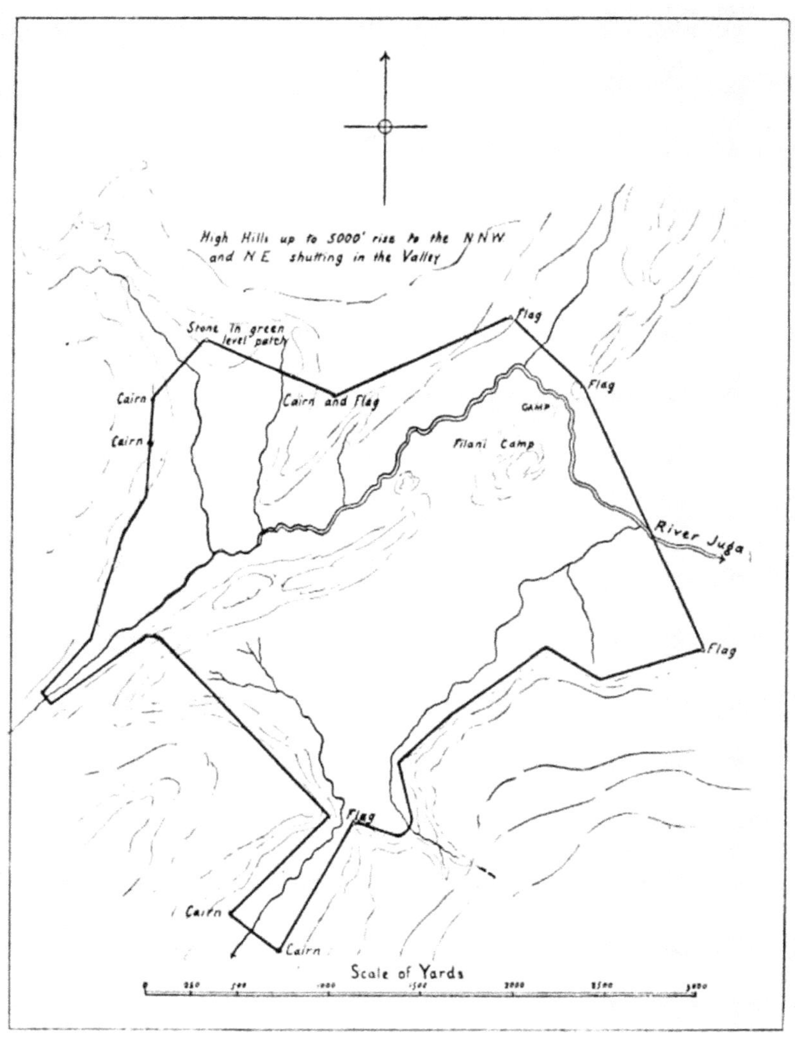

255 JUGA DISTRICT

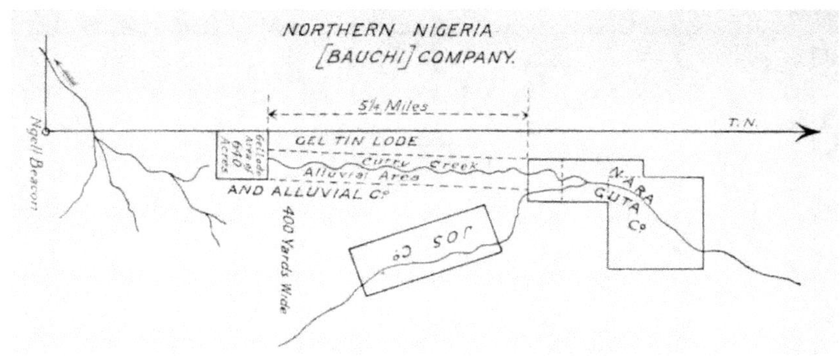

256 GEL TIN LODE AND ALLUVIAL CO. LTD.

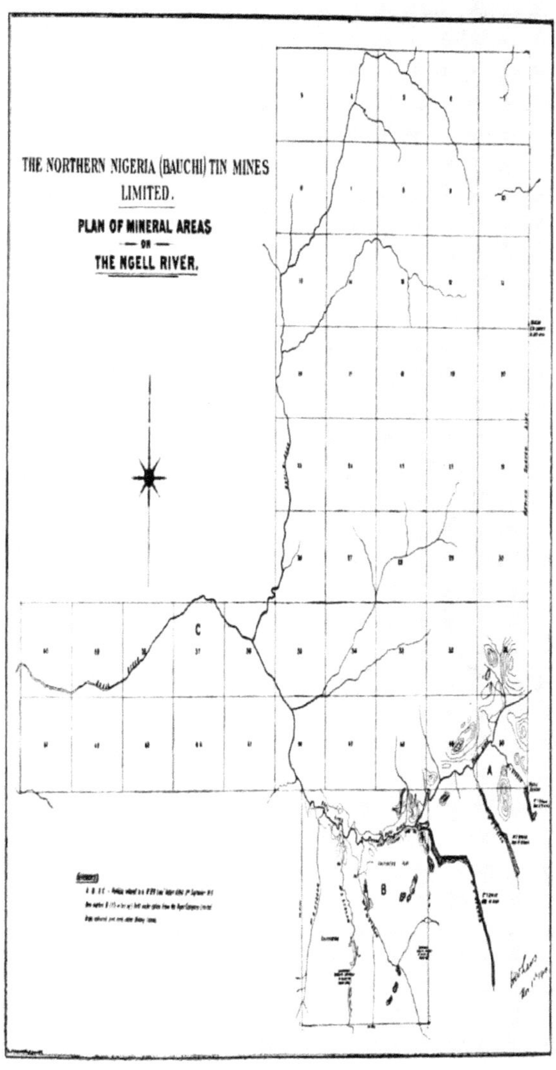

257 THE NORTHERN NIGERIA (BAUCHI) TIN MINES, LTD.

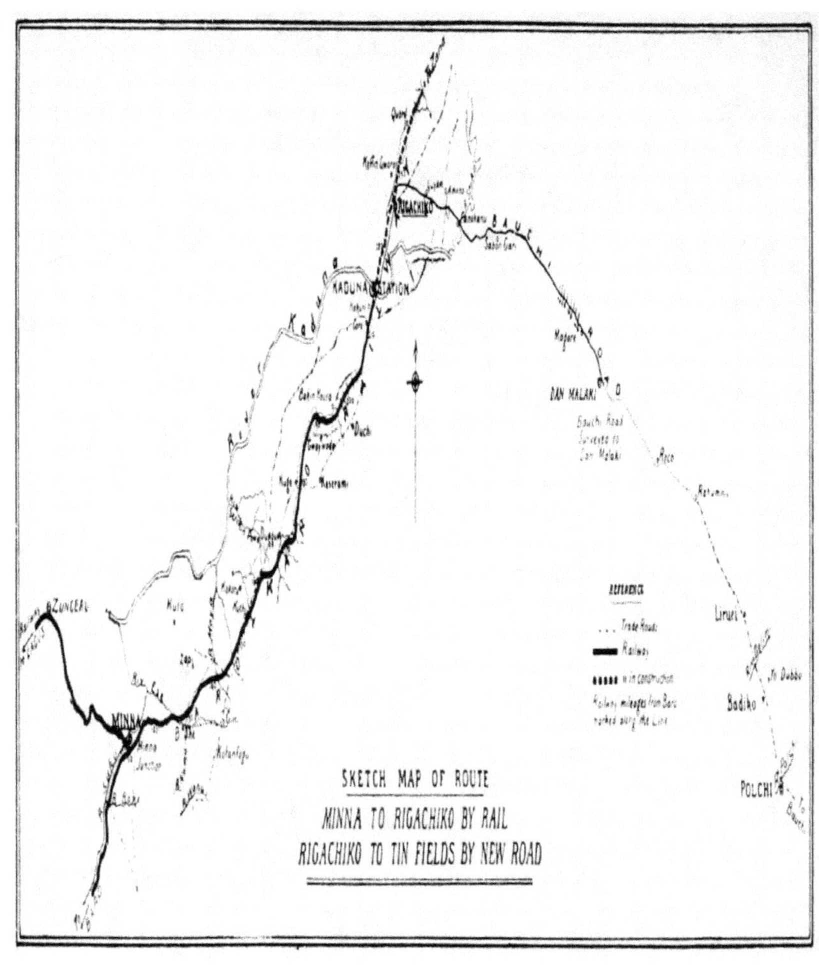

258 ROUTE FROM MINNA TO RIGACHIKO BY RAIL, AND FROM RIGACHIKO TO BAUCHI TIN FIELDS BY NEW ROAD

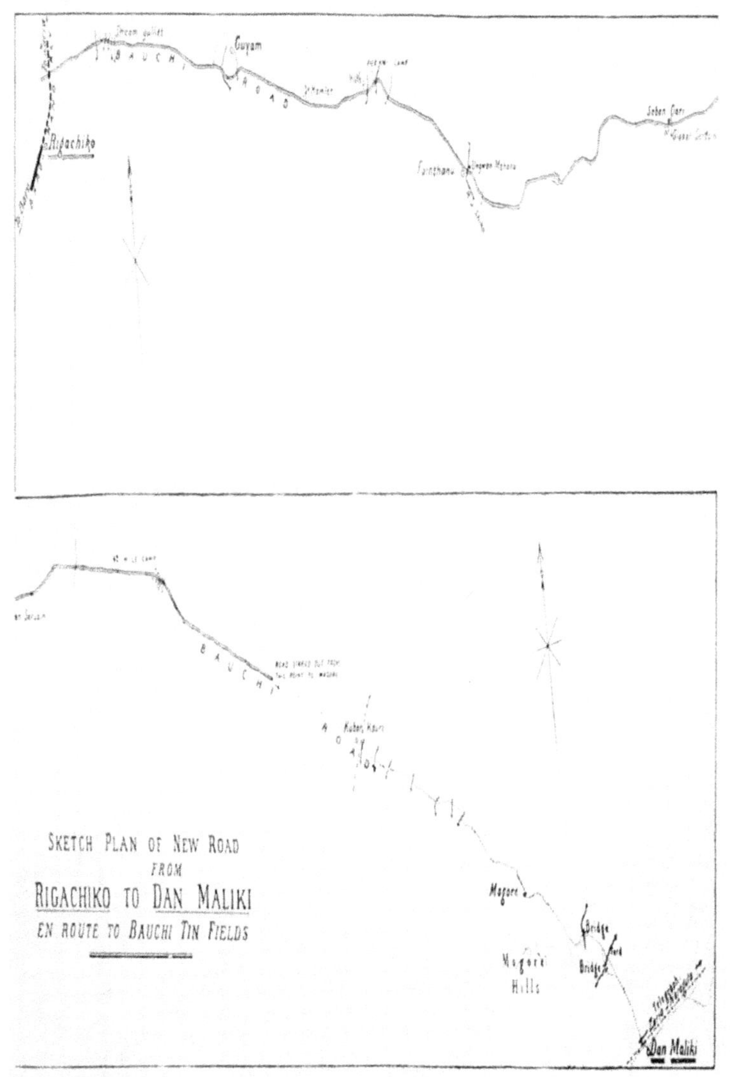

259 PLAN OF NEW ROAD FROM RAILWAY AT RIGACHIKO TO DAN MALIKI EN ROUTE TO THE BAUCHI TIN FIELDS